Karen Emerson
2019

Why Readers Are Raving About
Karen Emenheiser and *Unbecoming*

"Karen Emenheiser's *Unbecoming* explores the often-forgotten truth that before we can become the person we want, we have to unbecome many of the dysfunctional aspects of our personalities we have adopted over the years. In these pages, you'll discover how to unbecome your shortcomings to embrace with confidence the destiny you've always wanted."

— Patrick Snow, Publishing Coach and Best-Selling Author of
Creating Your Own Destiny and *Boy Entrepreneur*

"Karen Emenheiser's refreshing, down-to-earth, all-her-faults-exposed writing style makes the process of unbecoming easier for everyone because we know she's human and in it with us. Whether helping us build confidence, ban shame from our lives, improve our marriages, or learn to shed our light on others, *Unbecoming* gets into the dark nooks and crannies of our lives to help us bring our true, best, and brightest selves forth."

— Tyler R. Tichelaar, PhD and Award-Winning Author of
Narrow Lives and *The Best Place*

"Describing Karen Emenheiser could be a book on its own, but the basics of Karen's skills are evident in her every day, well-worn path. Karen's dedication to self-insight, continual growth, and following a true compass is the foundation of her empathy with others; she shows great discernment in care and a dedication to partner with others in their journeys. She is thoughtful and forthright."

— D. J. Dunlap, PhD

"I have witnessed the exceptional contributions Karen has made to our local Military community through her work as a counselor. She has not only dedicated herself to her profession but to enriching the lives of our Marines, Sailors, and families. Her non-judgmental, caring, and encouraging manner has proven vital in her commitment to helping and ensuring the wellbeing of others."

— Colonel, Infantry Regiment Commander,
United States Marine Corps

"Karen Emenheiser is smart, witty, positive, sharp as a tack, and most of all, she loves her Soldier and her Family. She has been a superb advisor to Soldiers' spouses as her husband rose in the ranks, and as I've watched her over the years, I've seen that she thrives on helping others be better spouses, better people, and…well, just better. Karen is the real deal, and I can say without reservation that her book *Unbecoming* will be a success because she focuses on first things first: love and support your Soldier, take care of your family, be positive, learn more every day, and help others succeed. Read this book! You will be better for it."

— Bill McCoy, Major General, United States Army (Retired)

"As a new military spouse, I was initially insecure and hesitant about my role as a wife and a senior Spouse. With Karen's guidance, I was able to overcome my timidity while she helped me navigate the difficult waters of military life. I am grateful to Karen for her patience, leadership, and indispensable friendship."

— Melanie Stokes, Military Spouse

"A great leader is said to be defined by two main characteristics: their authority (the capacity for meaningful action) and vulnerability (the willingness to be exposed to meaningful risk). Authority and Vulnerability are available for all to be learned, and can be found in *Unbecoming*. Here, Karen shares the uncertainty she has faced, the risks she has taken, and the emotional exposure she has endured on her road to living a life with purpose, close and meaningful relationships, and joy. Driven by her strong faith in God and commitment to a process of self-growth, she provides insights into how she has discovered her truer self, becoming a leader in her own right with a heart to be in the service of others."

— Raul T. Sabat, Licensed Marriage and Family Therapist

"Karen's ability to listen, understand, and guide with enthusiastic, straightforward advice is unmatched. Her desire to help others is one of the things I most admire. She truly cares about people no matter the situation. I am so thankful to have her as a 'go to' in my life!"

— Jillian Todd, Military Spouse

"Karen has the ability to see a situation, observe it, process it, and then share a deeper insight than anyone else I have met. I believe it is her life experiences combined with her own natural gift that allows her the ability not only to understand but to give great guidance. She does this through her wealth of knowledge gained through education, paying attention to life's lessons, and her amazing sixth sense."

— Nancy Harris, Military Spouse

"Karen Emenheiser is a gifted therapist who cares deeply for the well-being of her clients. She is a strong advocate for military families."

— M. Garrett, EdD, Military Spouse and Counselor Educator

"To whom does a Chaplain turn when they need to feel heard and valued? Besides the obvious answer, God, I also turned to Karen, during a time of sorrow and grief. In her I found a calm listener and compassionate counselor. She consistently provided the same exceptional care and wisdom for my Marines and their spouses during some of their darkest moments. You would be hard pressed to find a counselor of Karen's caliber or grace."

— Chaplain Len Driskell, Lieutenant, United States Navy

"Karen is a consummate professional. Her understanding of human nature and motivation is uncanny. When I need advice, motivation, or just to be heard, I go to Karen."

— Dr. Kassandra Engfer, Adjunct Lecturer of Psychology, Hawaii Pacific University and Military Life Counselor

Starting Over the Right Way

Unbecoming

How to Find the Courage and Confidence
to Live an Amazing Life

Karen Emenheiser, LCSW

AVIVA
PUBLISHING
New York

Unbecoming: How to Find the Courage and Confidence to Live an Amazing Life

Published by:
Aviva Publishing
Lake Placid, NY, USA
(515) 523-1320
www.AvivaPubs.com

Karen Emenheiser, LLC
karen@karenemenheiser.com
www.karenemenheiser.com

ISBN: 9781947937994
Library of Congress Control Number: 2019902426
Editors: Tyler Tichelaar and Larry Alexander, Superior Book Productions
Cover Designer and Interior Book Designer: Nicole Gabriel, Angel Dog Productions
Author Photo: Caroline Wilhite Photography LLC

Every attempt has been made to source properly all quotes.
Printed in the United States of America

"If we knew each other's secrets, what comforts we should find."

— John Churton Collins

To Barrett, for making my healing possible

Acknowledgments

Thank you to Patrick Snow for encouraging me every step of the way along my book writing journey. Thank you Tyler Tichelaar and Larry Alexander for taking care of my audience and making sure that I am heard accurately and cause only healing for my readers. Thank you to Nicole Gabriel for adding the artistic touches and making it special. Thank you to Susan Friedmann for getting excited with me and keeping in such close touch during the process. Thank you Raul for being my daily sanity check and inspiring so much of this book. Many Mahalos to my friends who cheered me on along the way and believed in me, particularly Kassandra and Erik. Thank you DJ for always knowing I had it in me. Thank you to my mom for being my biggest fan and connecting me to God. Thank you to my dad, who taught me resiliency and how to be a coach. And most importantly, my thanks to my clients who have stepped into my office with hopes of healing and growing past the pain. You are wise, proactive, and brave. You keep me inspired.

Contents

Preface

I never set out to write a Christian book. I'm definitely the last person who should be modeling good Christian thoughts and behaviors. Don't get me wrong; I love the Lord, but I'm a terrible Christian. I was just going to write a basic "how to be the best you" kind of book, based on my personal experiences and professional observations. But grace kept creeping in. How could it not? I don't know about you, but I don't stand a chance of being anything of much good without it. So, why am I a terrible Christian?

Growing up, we attended church pretty regularly until I was about eleven. For the next couple of years, we attended irregularly, I assume because of the health problems my parents were experiencing. My mother was diagnosed with multiple sclerosis around the same year my dad had a massive heart attack. Each were in their forties. I'm certain it helps to have an extra day of resting at home when your body is betraying you.

What I remember about going to church during this time was that I started to feel like a stranger in a foreign land. We went to Sunday school so infrequently that I couldn't keep up with the other kids. They would play speed memory games to learn the order of the books of the Bible. I never, ever knew my shit. It was embarrassing. All the other kids were encouraged to study week to week and remember what they had learned the week prior. They tore up the competition every Sunday morning. Every other kid but me. I also began to notice the difference in these kids and some of the little turds I went to public school with. They had learned how to act properly. They didn't tease each other or torment the teacher. I was a stranger in a foreign land, wishing I could be more like "them."

I knew the Lord; I loved the Lord. I got that from church camp and Vacation Bible School. Those programs gave me experiences that made me fall in love with our Creator. They spoke Truth to my heart that was undeniable and connected me to my soul's longing. He was never far from me, and I spoke with Him at least weekly, well into my twenties. And by "spoke," I mean begging for my way much of the time. It was an interesting walk with my Father, but one that would grow my faith and dependence on Him more and more every passing year. He revealed Himself to me through my struggles and pain, *proving* Himself worthy of all my trust. He revealed Himself in the "aha" moments following my torment when I was able to see the plan in retrospect—a plan that was always in my best interest and better than I could imagine. Oh, how I grew to love Him from childhood into adulthood. I just didn't know how to act. I didn't know the rules, how to pronounce names like Zaphnath-Paaneah, how to pray in front of others, or how to impress people with my knowledge of where to find which verse. I only knew how to be me, talk to Him, and love Him. Huh. Maybe that *was* the plan all along?

Introduction

Your Journey to a Better Life
with Less Drama

From the time we're born, we are told what to believe, how to be, and what we are: You're a feisty one; you're gonna be a heart-breaker; you're the shy one; you're just like your father. The story of us has begun to be told, and it becomes our unique identity that we tend to blindingly embrace. These identities can become hindrances to reaching our full potential as we try to act congruently with the story we have embraced. Crises arise when the image we've clung to is threatened through relationships of all kinds, encounters with others, accidents, traumatic experiences, milestones, transitions, aging, and loss. When our self-image is solid, desirable, and supported by our environment and others, our mental and emotional health feels balanced, and we are at peace. Other times, we feel shaky, unsure, and anxiety-ridden.

Sometimes I can't stand Christian music. I just really want some *gangsta* rap. But if I play it, what will my Christian friends think? What if my colleagues find out I flunked out of college? What if my daughters discover I've been charged with disorderly conduct—twice? What if my husband finds out that the strong, attractive woman he fell for was once ugly and tolerated abusive boyfriends? What if God heard me talk to my child the way I just did? What if my friends read this book and find out I'm really unsure of myself and not always as confident as I seem? What if my bully learns I don't really plan to kick her ass; I just want her to stop thinking me inadequate? All this self-exposure. All these people to let down! Can I just move to a deserted island, please?

Everyone is making me a failure!

Do you ever compare yourself to others? Wonder if you're good enough? Wish you could be "better"? Feel ashamed of your moments or areas of weakness? Surprise yourself by the reactions other people "cause" in you? *Other people* sure can really mess with your contentment, can't they? I'm not here to tell you how to improve yourself so much as I'd like to help you heal yourself. Improvement flows when healing has happened. This may take some unbecoming on your part: putting away regrets, shedding false ideas of yourself, and altering your beliefs about what makes you valuable. To heal is to become less reactive to sore spots or *emotional wounds.* These invisible wounds happened at times of rejection, abandonment, powerlessness, disappointment…. When we are healed, we can begin to grow and evolve into what is meant for us: wisdom, compassion, peace of mind, and joy.

Healing is sort of like renovating a house. Working on the foundation versus hanging new shutters is not about improving the image; it's about attaining a lasting place of security. Improving a home is often cosmetic or superficial, but I'm going for a deep, foundational inspection. Guess what? There are cracks in all of us, and they can be filled, but only if we are willing to look at them. These cracks are, in large part, emotional wounds. We are tempted to "paint," "clean," and "cover" the structural damage, or just put up signs like "Keep Out," "No Trespassing," or "Beware of Dog." Healing requires "unbecoming your walls" and getting to the root of who you really are before you begin to rebuild.

This situation of being human is uncomfortable to say the least. And there's not a whole lot you can do about it. I'd like to check out some misconceptions with you and help you find peace of mind in the midst of the struggle. I'm not perfect and never have been, but I'd like to think I'm healing and improving. You can begin that same quest when you can stop seeing your experiences as *defining* who you are. Once you escape shame and self-doubt, you can begin to evolve toward what God had in mind for you as God's creation. We do this in relationship to God and others. But I get that people can suck; I really do. I, too, am tempted to uphold an image or hide from people, depending on the day or mood I'm in. My buttons get pushed, I react to unhealed wounds, and I blame and get angry at others for pushing them. But at the end of the day, I'm the one responsible for healing what gets triggered, and you are responsible for your trigger responses. We need to look at them, heal them, and talk about them.

As a licensed clinical therapist for twenty years, and having friends who have bravely shared their vulnerabilities, I know I am not alone in this quest for peace of mind and comfort in my own skin. I've heard countless stories of folks trapped by shame and self-doubt and the experiences that got them there. I refer to these experiences as traumatic and simply non-nurturing events that made you question your view of yourself and your vision for your future. They can range from seemingly trivial to shocking, but they can always profoundly affect us.

The appearance that everyone else has it all together creates an even more keen uncertainty and loneliness. Sometimes we get married expecting a certain void to be filled, so we end up disappointed when the fairy tale ends. People come to me with many misconceptions about marriage, but the most common is that they are supposed to be "happy" all the time. Truth is, no relationship will expose you in ways you hate more than your relationship with your most intimate partner. This is because intimacy requires a vulnerability of exposing your insecurities to another. Defenses and distancing techniques are often go-to devices to avoid that sort of exposure.

We'll talk quite a bit about the ego in this book. We all have an ego, but it is really only a false sense of our self. It's the story of us that evolves over time, changing and growing with our experiences, achievements, comparisons with others, and so on. It's the part of us that makes us proud one day and self-loathing the next. It's a false identity, but we will go to great lengths to support it, some more than others, and it causes much strife in the world and in our personal lives. Ego is not our God-given identity, which is our genuine, authentic self, that is loved by God (and maybe our mama) "as is," and not based on where you've been, where you're going, or what you do. Rather, it's the identity that requires other people's and our own approval and acceptance.

We'll talk a lot about triggers in this book. Triggers are the alarm systems meant to help protect our safety, and at times, our ego. They cause an involuntary reaction that often doesn't match the actual stimulus, for example, overreacting to a comment, crying when it's inappropriate or unexpected, lashing out at our child, or shutting down in an uncomfortable situation. Triggers ignite a fight-or-flight response and can be identified, managed, and explained to others when we react in embarrassing ways. Triggers are formed throughout life by traumatic experiences, both large and small. They cause us to "self-protect" by withdrawing, shutting down, or lashing out, among other negative responses. People aren't being assholes so much as they are anxious or have been triggered.

We'll talk about assholes. Excuse my language (this will be the last time I ask), but some people are just downright assholes. Give the benefit of the doubt whenever you can; don't be quick to label an asshole just because they currently lack maturity, behave from triggered responses, or are ignorant about a subject. Once you do that, that person doesn't stand a chance with you and will always make you angry. That's a sucky place to be when said person is your new daughter-in-law, mother-in-law, coworker, or worse yet, spouse. But alas, we will talk about forgiveness, what it actually means, and how you don't have to dwell on what assholes do and/ or say. It doesn't change the fact that they are assholes—you just stop ruminating about it. And, oh yeah, you can be an asshole too. Am I right?

Finally, we will discuss the power of "now" throughout these pages and how it is a cure for almost every "problem" you have. It's the opposite of ruminating. It's getting out of your head and social media completely and paying attention to your life. Your life is this moment, and surprisingly, you have few to no problems when actually living your life. Problems exist in the timeline in your head—thinking about either what's already happened or what could happen in the future. Problems also exist in the judgments we make when watching other people's experiences (media, newsfeed, and blogs). As a species, we spend way too much time in our heads and on our phones, not dealing with what is right in front of us. A problem-free moment—that is your life, and that is where God exists.

To God, you are precious gem. You are born in perfect packaging and spend your early life showing off and adding to your handsome gift wrap. The gift that is you sure is pretty. The packaging may be quite gorgeous. You may not be perfect, but some parts of you are freaking awesome. Anyway, we were never meant to stay wrapped beautifully. The real gift is the jewel inside. It cannot be discovered until life begins to unwrap it. Many of us notice the gift wrap deteriorating around midlife and work hard to tape pieces back on, tie the bows tighter, or somehow polish the dulling colors of our packaging. We scurry in pursuit of updated packaging. It's a daunting pursuit that usually means we don't understand that the real gift is inside. The real value. The real self. And also, because a facelift is $10,000, y'all. The inside gift eventually becomes that fragile, wise, authentic, elderly person whose surrendered their packaging and begun to let the light of their gem shine. If you've ever worked in a nursing home, you know what I'm talking about.

A lot of years can be wasted working hard to remain in our tidy, neatly wrapped box. Sometimes people and experiences threaten to expose the cover up; other times, people support the story of you written in the wrapping. It's your *image* or *ego*. What you tell yourself and others you are is based on your life experiences. Not the present, but what we *present*. We need to unwrap, die to self, and *unbecome*. The military knows it has to break you down before rebuilding you—shedding the doubts and fears you were made to believe prior to boot camp. The bodybuilder knows the muscles have to be broken down before growing. The gardener knows the branches need pruning before the abundance of fruit appears.

I hope you have someone you feel loves you "flaws and all." Someone with whom you can be totally exposed and unconditionally loved without worrying what you said or might do to ruin it. For me, that is God and my parents. My husband would say he's another, but I haven't fully embraced that yet, and it's okay. We're only sixteen years in, and we are still building trust and working on expressing acceptance of each other. It's a process, and it's one we are both committed to. If you don't feel like you have that in your life, let me suggest you get to know this God that I know. Stop looking for things and people to fill a void that only your Creator can fill. God put that longing in you so that you would seek God. No one wants you to heal more than God does.

I believe in you; I only warn you against the thoughts of doubt and shame that may arise from reading this book. I hope they are not as strong as the ones that flowed through me while writing it. This has been my biggest risk yet. But I am determined to be unapologetically me while I walk closely with God toward becoming the best version of me. Are you?

Chapter 1

Braving "Relationsh*ts"

"I guess it comes down to a simple choice, really.
Get busy living, or get busy dying."

— Andy, *The Shawshank Redemption*

Before we can ever find true joy and inner peace, we must face, examine, and question the relationships that, like mirrors, show us who we *are*. Each person we encounter is a mirror staring back at us, reflecting us through their own eyes. It's exhilarating at times and humiliating at others. Our beliefs about our entire worth, purpose, and value can easily be swayed on a day-to-day basis depending on whom we hang out with that day. Recognizing this phenomenon and questioning its accuracy are the beginning steps toward how fully we embrace life, adventure, commitment, relationships, passions, and risks.

It is my belief that how well you brave relationships will propel you into living large or living in hiding. It will make the difference between getting busy living and getting busy dying. In this chapter, we will explore the courage it takes to face these reflections, question their validity, and begin to "brave-up" for the rest of the lessons this book offers.

WHY BOTHER?

We were created to desire being a part of something greater than ourselves. This may be a community, a sports team, a marriage, a fraternity, or part of the unfolding of God's plan for the world. Finding a spot for which we feel we were handpicked adds meaning and purpose to life. Even folks who spend a lot of time alone participate in adding to the greater good by recycling, doing a kind deed for a neighbor, or giving encouraging feedback to people on Facebook. As part of the group—household or planet—we gain a sense of contributing to goodness everywhere. Ultimately, this unity will help love win in the end.

But love will require sacrifice. In many relationships, that sacrifice will be our own selfish desires—we will give up the convenience of chucking a plastic bottle in the trash bin, we will miss gym class to give a friend a ride, we will put down the phone to really hear about our child's new discovery, and we will resist the need to be right and choose to be kind.

Do you want to become more loving? Chances are you want to leave this world a better place than what it was when you got here, have your children remember you fondly, and die without regrets. In accomplishing this, you will touch many lives and contribute to a greater good so big no one person could alter it alone. The effect of your loving presence could last generations. In the book *Seven Levels of Intimacy*, Matthew Kelly describes our essential purpose as being the best version of ourselves. We simply cannot do this in isolation. Although if we were left alone on an island, we would be pretty perfect—no temptation—it's not a true reflection of who we are because the truth comes from relationship. And the truth… is kind of ugly. If we could be honest with ourselves for a minute, we would see that we want to win; we want to look better than, be smarter than, and be higher than. We say we want more love and light, and yet we are compelled by darkness—urges to look perfect, intimidate, and impress. We want to be loving, but there's always that damn fuse—the short one, and the PMS, our competitive side, and hurrying to get to where we need to be. It's the spirit versus flesh competition that's been around forever. This is why we need relationship with God, too—God moves us to be more selfless.

Shortly after I got married, I attended a Bible study that always felt to me like a course in what I was supposed to look like. These good and rooted women often held up mirrors around me that reflected "you don't belong." Ever feel that way in a religious situation? It wasn't because of how they treated me or because they weren't lovely people. It was because I felt inferior. I was half-scared I'd drop the f-bomb, half-mortified that although I have loved my Lord since childhood, I have also been impatient, snarky, and sometimes downright rude. One day, our Bible study leader asked for prayers because she felt herself become slightly hostile with the FedEx delivery man for damaging her purchase. I remember clearly and distinctly the shame I felt for being such a loser Christian. She was such a delightful person with such small confessions. I vowed to try harder to hide my inner-beast.

I went home that night and cried, focusing my anger toward God and myself onto my husband, questioning why the hell I wasn't a better Christian yet? I wanted to be a lovely, passive, gentle, and kind person like all the other ladies! I was grieving my more aggressive demeanor and impatience with people. "I'm supposed to be the light of the world. When does *that* happen?" I asked him.

I could see my husband searching his mind desperately for an answer that might soothe me. That's when it hit me like a bolt of lightning right in my heart and out of nowhere: "My Grace is sufficient for thee." It just popped into my crazed brain and stopped me in my tracks. It was God's mercy and love letting me off the hook. Not a "try harder," not a "hang in there; you'll get it." But a genuine, "You are off the hook."

When we know we are okay, or off the hook, we become empowered to be real with others, in part because their opinions of us don't anger us. We may consider them, but they don't mess with our peace. It's the striving to be something we are not or something better than we are that makes relationships tiring. People you choose to spend time with will be those who reflect back to you an image you can bear. Everyone else becomes the enemy. If this book does nothing else for you, I hope it convinces you to step out of shame and be yourself—broken, imperfect, and unapologetically you. Then you can begin to enjoy relationships rather than reject them. Participate fully in life, becoming a better version of yourself, and help others become better versions of themselves. Then perhaps we can leave the world a better place for having been in it.

ON YOUR FEET, SOLDIER!

As a military spouse, I've moved nine times in fifteen years. I spent a lot of my thirties and half of my forties figuring out female relationships. Every move is fraught with fear of rejection, pressure to "find your tribe," and loneliness, at least for a while. Get good at making friends, or face isolation. All the while, I was riding the randomly shifting waves of uncertainty that are marriage, balancing past relationships without the benefit of daily contact, and keeping ties with my family so far away. I was mentally and emotionally exhausted. When relationships are perceived as going well, peace of mind and thoughts of competence and control ensue. When there appears to be something off, you could lose some sleep; am I right?

And sometimes, you think all is well, only to be blindsided with accusations of disloyalty, inattentiveness, and betrayal. Maybe you are the one feeling betrayed. It's insidious and deceitful at times, the feelings other people "cause" in us. Other times, it's a gut instinct telling us something we should have been aware of for a long time. Maybe we'll be brave enough to take these feelings and check them out, only to have them minimized, belittled, or ignored, and we now have a recipe for becoming hermits, or worse—suicidal. We will talk about making friends in upcoming chapters. It's a skill, and you can learn it.

Relationships are ridiculously hard. So ridiculous that I have come to anticipate perfect relationships in Heaven above—no pain, streets of gold, meeting my ancestors, and eating whatever I want without getting fat. I fantasize about a time when we can know and be known for who we truly are, without shame or misunderstanding. This quest for intimacy is one we all seek, but it often leads to self-loathing. Expressing your thoughts is hard. Expressing your vulnerabilities is a small miracle. This happens because there is a deceiver at work in both the communicator and the receiver. I know the deceiver as Satan; for you, it may be negative energy, depressive thoughts, the sound of someone's voice from your past that still plays in your head. How does the deceiver work? We know from Satan's interaction with Eve in the book of Genesis that the serpent asked her a question that made her doubt everything she knew to be true. On this earth, we are all subject to that deceitful line of questioning: Do they really like you, or are they just flattering you? When they said they miss their old friends, does that mean they don't value your friendship? The teacher probably praises all students that way; do you think you're special? Did that person just look at you and roll their eyes? Are they whispering about you? They do it because they want you to believe you are nothing, a nobody. They use other people to impress that upon us. They use our insecurities to make us believe it already exists, and any person we relate to on any given day could expose it: our lack of self-worth, value, or purpose.

Questions and doubt can drive you mad. Sometimes people actually are annoyed by you, and sometimes you're being duped. How can you tell? And why does it matter? Later in this book, we will talk about skills to navigate relationships when the evil one wants you confused, in hiding, and failing in love. But first, we will confront, head on, the ridiculousness of being in this broken world where we are faced with wanting to be known and loved by imperfect people with their own insecurities and the insane amount of courage it takes to press forward. No mind-reading, little benefit of the doubt, unforgiveness, disgrace, mercilessness, ingratitude, competitiveness, and arrogance are abounding—they are all around us, and let's face it, within us. It's enough to make you seethe with hatred for humankind.

So why bother? Partly, because not all human contact can be avoided. Practice makes perfect is enough for some folks to jump in. Others are compelled by Scripture to love one another. Others may just be extroverts who can't help themselves—they have to get involved with people. Some people understand that there's a lot of pain and anguish and anxiety beneath a lot of ugly, rude behavior, so they tolerate all kinds of people and behaviors well. I happen to be an extrovert. I get energy from people. Introverts tend to find socializing more draining and need solitude to recharge. I feel alive when relationships are going well and haunted when they feel wonky. But both personality types need connection with others at some level. If you would like to know which type you are, ask yourself two basic questions:

1. When a social function I have been looking forward to is suddenly cancelled, am I secretly relieved or am I disappointed?
2. Would I rather spend the day in a room by myself or in a room full of (friendly) strangers?

Whichever you identify with most, avoiding human connection, even with those people who are a struggle, can lead to feelings of incompetence, loneliness, isolation, regret, repressed growth, or worse, death. Our enemy is counting on these things occurring.

When I first became a Military Spouse, my husband told me I was expected to attend certain social Spouse functions. My exact response: "Oh, I don't do that," meaning, "I don't do fake, forced, female friendships." I'll never forget the deer-in-the-headlights look that fell over his face. I soon realized that supporting him meant learning the social ropes so I could eventually host these types of gatherings as he climbed the ranks. It meant finding friends who were married to his peers. It meant learning to cope with some very rude behaviors. I almost quit putting myself out there, but because I didn't, I grew. Just last week, I was attending a Spouse function. A woman I later found out was a General's wife walked straight up to me, stared me in the face, and said, "Oh, you look different," cupped her friend's ear with her hand and whispered into it, and then walked away. I looked at the woman next to me and said, "Did that just happen?" She nodded, lips pursed together. And we belly-laughed for the next five minutes. Growth.

MATTERS OF THE HEART

For at least most of us, marriage just seems like an expected step in adulthood, after education and employment. When you reach a certain age, everyone around you seems to be counting on you "settling down." Often, there is also internal pressure to check that box for whatever reason. As a therapist, I work with young Military members, who often see marriage as a way of getting out of crappy barracks and into a two-bedroom home. They have the income to support a marriage and feel ready by virtue of their experiences, training, and surroundings. Statistics show this population marries younger, and inevitably, divorces at much higher rates. I don't mean to sound discouraging or patronizing to this cohort—I am in full support of making these marriages work; it's my passion and what I get paid to do. It just also happens to be ridiculous to think it could work without support, encouragement, and balls of steel.

Let me explain. Basically, the longer I'm married and I counsel couples, the more aware I am of how absurd this perfect and beautiful concept of marriage is. How can it ever actually function in this fallen world, with broken people, from "different planets," and no handbook on knowing feelings, explaining feelings, delaying gratification, active listening, thinking before speaking, etc.? These are only a few of the necessities for making any relationship work, but particularly, marriage. I will talk more about this in Chapter 15 on marriage. I just want to validate here that, yes, relationships are hard.

Anything that grows, hurts.

But I'm going to try to help you. Sit tight.

You'll never truly know how damaged a person is until you try to love them.

People are often surprised that, as a marriage counselor with a successful and mature relationship, I once told my husband I hated him. Not bragging here, but yes indeed, I said, "I hate you." And not just once. This was in the beginning when my husband was my walking, full-length, circus mirror. The reflection was agonizing for me. Fuck you, mirror. I don't look like that.

Never one to shy away from giving advice or constructive criticism, or thinking through every action, or being slow to anger, or doing everything so damn neatly, my husband soon became my worst enemy. I had just spent seven months convincing him that I had no flaws so he would choose me. Obviously, I wanted to maintain that image, partly so I could keep his interest and partly because my ego depended upon it—the ego I sold him in under seven months: the time it took him to marry me after our introduction. I was flawless. I stood to lose him as well as my self-esteem if I were found out. If I were perfect, I'd win every argument, and never feel ashamed or embarrassed. In essence, I'd be worshipped. In the book *The Power of Now*, Eckhart Tolle calls this story of ourselves an *illusory identity*—a false sense of self, derived from guilt, shame, and regret. In my case, it was shame. I had a sense that every broken relationship was a result of my not being *good enough*. My impulsive, clumsy, loud nature was rearing its ugly head in front of a man who found these characteristics annoying. Shit got real. So long honeymoon period.

Every day in junior high, a boy I'll call Sheldon told me I was ugly. He'd sit in the desk in front me, daily turn around to me and ask me how I got so ugly. He was the bully straight out of a movie, looks and all. (This story doesn't end here. Look for it again in Chapter 13.) I had very thin hair, cystic acne, and I was once mistaken for a boy by my parents' friends. My ego response was to improve my looks, get an education, a suit, definitely a briefcase, taking no shit from anyone, and maybe even writing a book one day. I would prove myself worthy, looking to boys' attraction to me as validation it was working.

Relationship number one didn't go so well. At sixteen, I fell for a boy who convinced me that he'd be my boyfriend if I gave him my virginity. I did, and two days later, he dumped me and slept with my best friend. I'd love to tell you I didn't take that shit, but I became fixated on proving my worth by getting him back and keeping him for the next three years. He never changed, so I tried harder.

There was a string of similar relationships for the next fourteen years. There was the pathological liar who made me feel crazy for years. However, I became more determined to prove my worth as a woman, and finally, this did not include a man's desire. I had done some real badass things. Getting a master's degree was pretty badass in my family. Becoming director of a family therapy program at twenty-eight was pretty awesome. I couldn't understand why I was still single. I was marginally impressive, and to be honest, my standards were pretty low when it came to men. One night over a beer, I was lamenting to a fellow graduate student how a girl like me could still be single. John, being a sixty-five-year-old, wiser-type student, used a Bible verse to clear things up.

"Have you ever heard, 'Don't throw pearls before a swine'?"

"No."

"If you mix in precious pearls with slop, a pig will never discriminate the valuables from the crap. For the men you are choosing, a woman is a woman is a woman is a woman. They slop it all up without separating or even noticing the gems within. So why do you expect them to hold you in any sort of esteem?"

That's when I realized my worth—and never settled for mediocre again.

Okay, okay, I'm joking. It wasn't quite that simple. Truth is, there were multiple pigs after that. Pigs of my own choosing. I was the girl who dated men for their potential. I was an aspiring therapist, so I believed everyone had potential! It took a couple of decades to learn that people don't really change. Or at least we should never, ever assume they will.

When I met my husband, he actually took interest in my more esteemed attributes. I had a good physique, was educated, a boss, older than him, independent. These things mattered to him. He was choosy, and I had impressed him. In the beginning, I believe he fell in love with my attributes. What a shocker when we moved in together and my effed-upness came out. Effed-upness is my word for being an impulsive, careless, reckless, ugly redneck with average intelligence. It didn't help that he was perfect. He knew finances. He was a clean-cut, methodical officer in the United States Army. I had finally met someone who valued all my hard work and self-empowerment and how I had become a better version of myself. I wanted to see myself through those admiring eyes forever. Damn mirror. Eventually, for everyone in an intimate relationship, the masks must come off. For many, myself included, this can be terrifying and agonizing.

KNOW YOUR TRIGGERS

Relationships will never be perfect, or even neat and tidy. But they can be more functional. More enjoyable. To achieve that, you will need to understand how you've been wired in the first decades of your life. Why? Because the body stores certain experiences as *traumatic* and will catapult you into defense mode at the mere sniff of a similar threat. This information is stored in the amygdala: the fear center of our brain. The amygdala is primal, not at all rational, but incredibly well-intentioned. It alerts us to fight or flee from life-threatening situations. And thank God for it, particularly for my Neanderthal ancestors (a little known tidbit I got from a DNA website). A perceived threat without any notion of the actual potential danger only has to be reminiscent of past danger. Fourth of July fireworks to receiving a confrontational email can elicit intense physiological responses. The rational mind knows there is no threat, but the response does not. The reaction is *as if* a prior event is actually happening. It's completely irrational, leaving the experiencer feeling out of control.

The same phenomenon happens not only to combat veterans, but to almost anyone who has risked getting out of bed in the morning and facing the world. The amygdala sniffs out smoke in the heated argument with your spouse and friends. It sniffs out smoke from a social event you are dreading, a fear you are facing, the cues you are getting from your love interest or boss. The smoke may be *more evidence that you're incompetent, unworthy, invaluable, disgusting, pathetic,* or *worse.* These triggers don't get tapped in isolation. The sooner you can identify what triggers you have in a relationship, the more authentic and capable you will be in intimate relationships. You will go from "I hate you" to "I get triggered when you say that/do that/look at me like that." "I hate you" is unhelpful, dishonest, and usually, regretful. Trust me on that. You begin to feel out of control in your relationship and less likely to approve of yourself, which only perpetuates the cycle of denying the parts of yourself that are "bad." But knowing your triggers and fears is the start to being able to unbecome.

RELATIONSHIPS ARE MESSY

Within a week of moving to Hawaii, we took our girls to the beach to play. I sat on my chair, and watched in awe as a local woman boogie-boarded with her daughter, her hair a mess, but looking tan and fit and full of life. I began to wonder if I belonged, if I'd ever take to the ocean with that kind of spirit. Then she did the unthinkable. She plunked her wet, thong-wearing-ass smack down on the beach a few yards away. I cringed at the thought of all the sand glued to her nether regions and the days it might take to de-grain completely. I looked at my toes and felt uncomfortable that the sand had made its way up my ankle. Ick. Why did I want my life to be mess-free? Neat and tidy? When did I outgrow the tomboy who got dirty and made memories? Where was my inner child? I told myself right then and there, "My goal is to get messy and relish it—to live life to the fullest." Not that day, of course, but I'd slowly work to shed my tidy image so I could be adventurous again. My kids would be thrilled.

RELATIONSHIPS ARE ART

You are creating and getting messy in the process of relating. There will be times when you will trip over your words and feel completely misunderstood and awkward. Then you will dig a little deeper. You will find the right words; they will connect to the receiver, but they, unfortunately, will misunderstand. You will sense their unease; you will propose another way. You will decide to just hug, or agree to disagree, or perhaps, you will create a platform on which to stand as a couple. Either way, it's moving, changing, unfolding, and based purely on the words or movements you use to make yourself known to another human being who can't read your mind and has their own selfish motives. Ridiculous, right? I'm never surprised to hear a Service Member confess they'd rather be in the field or even back on a long deployment, where life is simple, relationships are black and white, and conversations are clear and straightforward. Love relationships are messy as hell. The good news is we have tools to mop up the mess. These tools are grace, mercy, forgiveness, and make-up sex, to name a few.

Kintsukuroi is the Japanese art of repairing broken pottery. Using a pure gold resin mixed with lacquer, the artist puts the pieces back together. The streak of gold defines the repaired line, rather than simply disguising it. It treats the breakage as part of the history of the object and the repair as valuable to its history. In essence, the broken and repaired pottery becomes much more exceptional, interesting, cared for, and valuable than it was in its original form. These are the touches of

God in us—our own use of grace, mercy, and forgiveness in our broken relationships. Repairing a broken treasure becomes a beautiful display of art dependent upon the work of two or more spirits working collaboratively to clean up the mess.

SUMMARY

"I'm scared that I'm not myself in here, and I'm scared that I am."

— Piper, *Orange Is the New Black*

In the show *Orange Is the New Black*, Piper is a public relations executive with a career and a fiancé. Then her past involvement with a drug-runner gets her sentenced to a minimum-security prison. In this new environment, she finds herself befriending the most unusual and unexpected people. Relationships expose parts of us we wouldn't otherwise see and compel us to look at ourselves and figure out who is looking back. I will probably always feel like my best self when I'm alone. I'm lovely, calm, and kindhearted. But the question remains: Is this the real me, or is it the crazy-lady I am as a wife, mother, and friend?

EXERCISE

1. Are there any relationships, past or present, that reflect a scary image of yourself—perhaps an image that makes you feel incompetent, ugly, or naïve?

    _____

    _____

    _____

    _____

    _____

    _____

2. In what ways can you allow the Grace of God to work in your life to let you off the hook?

_____

_____

_____

_____

3. List some examples of where you have been casting yourself before swine.

_____

_____

_____

_____

4. What areas in your life do you strive to improve? What ideas about yourself do you need to shed? How do you need to "un-become"?

_____

_____

_____

_____

5. When does your amygdala "smell smoke?"

_____

_____

_____

_____

Chapter 2

Committing to Your Choices

"Everything will be alright in the end so if it is not
alright it is not the end."

—Deborah Moggach, *The Best Exotic Marigold Hotel*

In Chapter 1, we talked about the absurdity of committed, adult relationships. In this chapter, we'll take a look at why you should consider sticking it out as well as other feats you are pursuing. I won't try to dissuade you from a decision to divorce or give up on any current aspiration—I'm not in your shoes. I just want to make a case for consideration before you make any big decisions. First, let's define choice: Webster's defines choice as, "selected as one's favorite or the best." Commitment also means staying loyal to what you said you were going to do long *after* the mood you said it in has left you. And that, to me, explains precisely why commitment is so undesirable.

THE LAND OF PLENTY

We live in a world where we have options—some argue we have too many. Theorists have proclaimed that too many options can be debilitating, rather than freeing. In a first-world arena, we are often encouraged to follow our dreams, find our gifts, and do what we love, and often, we are to do all this at around seventeen. Like what the hell does a seventeen-year-old know about anything? Nowhere in my life has this been clearer than during my work with Service Members who at some point come to believe they have made a huge mistake by joining the military. They act as if they had some understanding of their decision-making back when they signed up. Recruiters make a mean case for joining, and the alternatives are sometimes not too appealing. Add to that the fact that final brain formation is over a decade away and most choices are impulsive and very short-sighted, and it's hard to believe we as a culture put this expectation on our youth. This is true in marriage, housing, career decisions, investment choices, and shampoo, protein powder, salad dressing, and movie options. The land of plenty: plenty of room for the inevitable nagging thought that we could have chosen better.

As a therapist, I work hard to help people consider their long-term, best interests without convincing them to stick anything out. It's not my life to live or leave behind. But the compulsion to impress some commitment upon folks is like a lump in my throat squelched only by knowing a God of second, third, ninety-ninth chances who allows us to make a good life after every wrong turn. God can clean up any error and, as I know, one or two stellar, second-thought life decisions. Notice I said "decisions." Sometimes life circumstances lead to alternate life paths: layoffs, deaths, accidents. But I'm talking about the folks who, at some point on their journey, think, *Never mind; I want something else.* Some decisions to leave whatever you're leaving are brave. An abusive marriage, an oppressive job, a child you decide to bear and put up for adoption because you weren't ready. I'm talking about those opting out because they aren't happy or think they can't be after a short stab at the process. Committing a little while longer than you feel inclined to in marriage may carry great potential if you can understand the processes occurring in the first stages of "becoming one." Make no mistake, all these things require sacrifice and discomfort. And I think these are things we believe should be avoided at all costs or are signs that something has gone terribly wrong and cannot be remedied.

I typically see couples in the first five years of marriage with many hurt feelings and intense conflict related to how the other person is. Invariably, the first five years are about old wounds being tapped by one's partner; the client freaks out in some way, causing their partner to jump to their own defense, and the rest is history. I first normalize this process as trying to figure out their dance, but that they are stepping on each other's toes quite a bit. Good communication can rectify this and make the other more aware, but triggers and emotional wounds make good communication nearly impossible for any of us. The first five years is about healing these old wounds within this intimate relationship. If done correctly and with the help of a therapist, marriage can get a lot easier after this point, but folks don't normally recognize that. People are often disillusioned by what marriage offers them in the beginning, and they need to learn about the processes at work. Some fights will resolve in a few weeks—some will last years. Some people have deeper wounds creating a more severe relational post-traumatic stress response. The new, otherwise healthy, relationship uncovers these wounds; it doesn't cause them. These problems will exist in every relationship you encounter following the ones you trash because you are hurt. A trained counselor can see this dynamic play out and help the couple break free from it. A loving and committed relationship can heal all kinds of prior damage with the right guidance.

> "And endurance develops strength of character, and character strengthens our confident hope."

> — Romans 5:4

Happiness becomes a lot more unshakeable with confident hope. It's misguided to seek happiness first—unless you want the cheap, quick version that won't last long. Doing it right takes a lot of trust in the process. When I signed up to run a half-marathon, I had to build my endurance from the couch to 13.1 miles, one mile at a time. Eventually, I was out for ten-mile long runs every Saturday morning leading up to the race. You know what was the toughest part of those ten-mile practice runs? My house to the road. Not just was it mentally tough to get out the door, but I physically hurt more during the run down my driveway than I did at mile ten. My heart was faster, my breathing heavier during the sixteenth of a mile that was my driveway. Why? Because I hadn't adapted yet. My body was in shock by what I was setting out to do. If I didn't know any better, like how good I'd start to feel around mile three, I would have given up before I ever started. If something feels wrong, we are inclined to escape, avoid, or question the correctness of our choice. But perhaps we need to endure the pain of unbecoming before it feels right and solid. A muscle will break down before it grows...and it hurts like hell.

WHY STOP NOW?

If you've ever dieted for two weeks, started a bodybuilding regime, or made it halfway through a bad Netflix series, you may have agonized over this question: "Why stop now? Maybe there's more if I stick to it." While I'm giving you permission to stop wasting time on a mediocre Netflix series, many other ambitions should be pursued long and hard. Bad Netflix series, video games, and scrolling social media are only sapping up time and energy that could be better spent on self-improvement measures. Why self-improve? Because the world needs you. Your family needs you. They need you to be healthy. Also, don't you want to be successful, whatever that means to you? This takes commitment to the endeavor.

Albert Einstein said, "I have no special talents. I am just passionately curious." Curious people stick things out for the mere obsessive thought: *This road must lead somewhere. God must be up to something. Surely, I'll grow from this. There must be a point.* When we value the point of it all over immediate gratification, we stubbornly see things through. We wait expectantly on God to fulfill the promise of an abundant life. We trust the process to land us at the goal line, even when we can't see it clearly.

I am curious about the lives of people. Every life is a story with a beginning, a middle, and an end. I want to hear it all. My practicum supervisor in graduate school told me that we are all creating a tapestry with our lives. In the beginning, the threads are woven and chosen for you by the nature of those who brought you into this world, raised you, violated you, betrayed you, and encouraged you. At some point, usually around eighteen, you take over the seat of the artisan. It is then you have a choice to follow the same pattern and use what's in your tool bag. Or not. Much of it comes within our control to change things, pick a new pattern, and begin weaving in some finer fabrics. There are tools everywhere. In mentors, heroes, teachers, books, travel, and much more. The outcome is beautiful, and like every other art form, intriguing and mystifying.

A story—I want to hear about the black, junky fabric, how you chose a new way and then stuck with it until it overshadowed the darker parts of the tapestry, becoming something other than what you felt destined to become. If you've ever been up close to art you are creating, you know that once in a while you need to take a step back and see it all coming together. Persevering through the tedious brush strokes or redundant weaving loom, you can begin to see the whole picture coming together—a story of many colors connecting via commitment to the *process*. I want to hear the *whole* story of what will become of you—and what will unbecome of you.

GROWTH MINDSET VS. FIXED MINDSET

Some people lean more toward the view that interests are inherent in a person, simply waiting to be awakened or found—this is what we call a *fixed mindset of interest*. Others lean more toward the view that interests can be developed, and that, with commitment and investment, they can grow over time—we call this a *growth mindset of interest*. The results of a study reported in the *Harvard Business Review* in September 2018 as "Having a Growth Mindset Makes It Easier to Develop New Interests" found that undergrads with a growth mindset tended to remain interested in a passion even after it became complex and challenging. Their counterparts, students with a fixed mindset, tended to become uninterested in what they identified as a passion when it took a more cumbersome turn. I relate this to taking a statistics course as a requirement for my psychology major. This was not what I signed up for. I cheated my way through high school math and barely passed collegiate math with a D. Numbers are not my strong suit, but because, and only because, the course related to the field I was passionate about, did I endure the torture. But art and science coexist, and rarely will you find one without the other's influence. The authors of the article, Paul A. O'Keef, Carol Dweck, and Greg Walton, state "Innovation requires both reaching across fields and, often, acquiring more than a surface-level understanding of those fields." Having a growth mindset promotes this kind of resilience in any and all commitments, including relationships, as well as recovering from traumatic experiences. Viktor Frankl, a holocaust survivor and author of *Man's Search for Meaning* explains how we can find meaning and purpose in the most harrowing situations. These kinds of folks are actively searching for their personal growth and triumph, despite, or even because of, what has happened to them.

PICK SOMETHING AND STICK TO IT

The Military folks I see often have a point where they question their decision to enlist. "This isn't what I thought it was gonna be. I didn't sign up for this." From my viewpoint, with my teenage years twenty-five years behind me, I see the rest of their contract as a blink of time. It is something they will likely never regret completing. I understand not reenlisting, but backtracking from an agreement that would at least propel them into "something" better than where they came from makes me uneasy to say the least. "Stay the path!" I want to scream. Promotions and a better life are usually on the other side if you stick to something long enough. Not just financially, but you also get a sense of competence. Not many people start out as the rock star of their occupation, certainly not a Marine. Most steps toward committing to something make us feel like idiots in the beginning. Can you tolerate that feeling? When you understand that endurance eventually leads to a confident hope, you can better trust that process. When you understand that before age twenty-five, you can't know shit about what you want, then you realize that sometimes you just have to make a decision and stick with it. A question I like to ask my Marines when they are sitting in my office, checking out with the various services, as they approach the end of their contract is: Are you the same person you were four or five years ago? I have yet to get a yes to that question. Invariably, the answer is a vehement no. When asked to elaborate, they all profess some version of, "I am no longer that confused, selfish, undisciplined kid." They claim to have more direction and maturity. And they feel like they've made it.

DON'T CLOSE THE BOOK ON A BAD CHAPTER

Relationships and life have chapters, or seasons if you prefer. There is a saying, "If things are going badly, don't worry; they will get better! If things are going well, don't worry; they will get worse!" The sooner we learn that life is more of a roller-coaster ride than an easy downhill descent to happiness, success, and perfection, the more committed we will be to embracing the whole mess.

Erica came to see me a little over one year into her second marriage. Her first marriage had ended after about nine years, after she had lost interest in having the same fight over and over. Not surprising to me, she was recognizing that she was having the same fight with her current husband, so she had bravely sought help.

"Once again, I feel like I can't be myself in this relationship. He is so critical and rude. It seems like one day he likes me and the next he doesn't."

Upon further questioning, and later on, meeting with her and her husband Steve together, I learned that her husband is indeed imperfect and moody when under stress. Some communication-facilitating exposed a bit of a misrepresentation in comments based on Erica's old wounds and imagination. After a few sessions, it was easy to coach Steve into expressing his deep love for Erica, and I asked how he could better express himself to her when he was stressed. He was able to recognize and explain that when he feels stressed and things are out of his control, he micromanages her and the household and gets angry when things, "Don't go as they should, and I have little to no say...just like at work." Once Erica understood this, she softened and developed compassion for this man who was clearly covering up some vulnerable feelings. They hugged and agreed to try to make some room for each other's moods and not take them so personally, provide some soothing, if warranted, and most importantly, discuss the situation or reconnect at a later time.

Erica was able to say, "I feel like I take things very personally and jump to my own defense quite often. I feel as though I can have some compassion for him and maybe even soothe him by giving him some space or asking if I could do something for him to lighten his load."

Steve added, "I feel like I can't just go around spreading my pain, and I need to at least mention 'It's me, not you,' until I can get a better grip on my moods. I am trying. Please be patient with me."

I'm certain Steve got laid that night.

SUMMARY

Nothing is perfect. And *no one* is perfect. When we get to the chapters on banning shame and marriage, we will examine how to tolerate these feelings and trust the process. You can't be expected to make the perfect decision for a career or a spouse because no such thing exists. Success is closely tied with commitment, fighting the good fight, and going back for more. Some fights last twenty years, some one or two, before we iron them out or they burn out. God is always working on our behalf; we just need to trust God. But when we jump ship midway through the process, we don't give it a chance and risk losing a lot more. I believe with every quit we lose confidence—in ourselves, in others, and in God, making it that much harder to get in the game a second time.

EXERCISE

1. What do I need to commit to?

    _____

    _____

    _____

    _____

2. What help do I need to make this commitment?

    _____

    _____

    _____

    _____

3. In what ways can/will my situation improve over time?

    _____

    _____

    _____

    _____

4. In what ways can/will I improve over time in this situation?

    _____

    _____

    _____

    _____

Chapter 3

Getting in the Game

"I don't know where I'm going, but I'm on my way."

— Carl Sagan

Much of life is about going forward without a map, direction, or guide. We are feeling our way through the darkness. It's unnerving, but it's a fact of life. Whether you're just starting out or just starting over, your life is now. Not only do you need to make a choice and stick with it, but you need to do so in a timely manner. When you don't put yourself out there, the world is missing out. Particularly if you've been hurt! After all, *hearts are made by being broken.* You'll be kinder and more sympathetic toward others once you've experienced pain yourself, and we could use more compassionate, sensitive, and understanding folks among us.

#WHOWHATWHYWHEREWHEN?

Research says getting married before age twenty-five increases your risk of divorce. But wait too long and you'll have baggage and shriveling ovaries to contend with. I have seen people make hasty decisions to wed, but also flourish because of the standards they've invoked for their own choice for a mate as well as the commitment they expect to make and be made to them. I am no expert on what spouse is right for you, but because I know my standards and tastes changed between the time I was twenty-two and twenty-nine (when I actually got married), yours may too. However, it took me longer to grow up and get my standards straight than some. The brain isn't completely formed until age thirty, but biologically, the best reproductive age is much earlier than that. There is no way to time these things. I've worked with a number of young married couples, and although this demographic faces a potentially higher risk of hardship and divorce, with the proper guidance and maintenance, I am confident they can achieve lasting unions.

A friend of our family, Jordon, was eighteen when he got his high school sweetheart pregnant. They were in love, so they decided to get married and call it a family. A year later, she was pregnant with their second child, all before either of them could legally drink to deal with any of it! I was more than skeptical; I was cynical about their chances for success. I secretly shamed them in my mind, looking down at the ineptitude it takes to make such an idiotic decision. "What the hell were they thinking?" I would ask my sister, mom, husband, and friends. "Boy, wait till they really start to face life's problems. Poor stupid children." And I didn't mean their offspring; I meant them. But the more I hung out with this adorable couple who had a lot of family support and encouragement, the more I noticed just how freakin' happy they were. And in love. They doted on those babies and each other. They worked and saved, and just recently, they bought a house. Jordon and his wife's parents are in love with being grandparents. It wasn't my path, but just maybe, with commitment, they will make it. I'm rooting for honor, commitment, and kept promises for them.

My path was different. I chose poorly with relationships one, two, and three. Whereas Jordon fell for the sweet prom queen, I almost always sought out the misguided youth. But when I finally met my husband, I had standards, rules, and deal-breakers he needed to know.

1. I will not cohabitate out of wedlock.
2. I will not move for a boyfriend.
3. You need to have salvation and a relationship with God.
4. I'm not interested in another four-year boyfriend. Shit or get off the pot.

The chemistry was there, similar foundational values were there, and our backgrounds were closely related. What else do you need? Commitment. When folks tell me they need to live with someone prior to marriage to see how it works, I immediately question their faith in God, their willingness to commit during hard times, and their ability to make wise choices. Sorry, but it takes a level of faith, endurance, and discernment to commit to a person without having lived with them. I know because I asked my husband to make this decision, having known me for just five months, and only having been in my physical presence twenty-one days total from the time we met to the day we met at the altar. We put all faith in God to protect our marriage. We knew after a couple of months of dating that there weren't any serious red flags, and we did all the counseling that talked about all the shit life might throw at us and how we'd have to stay together anyway.

It was a shot in the dark for sure. For both of us. But with a foundation there, we took the risk. And we agreed that no matter what, no one was getting out of this relationship alive. We would talk, get counseling, and pray together if we had to. And you can be sure the baggage I was totin' had to make him wonder whether he hadn't just made the biggest mistake of his life. In the marriage chapter, we'll take a deeper look at how people heal and grow in relationships if done right. I am not the same basket-case I was the first five years in. And nothing has made me fall more in love with my husband than his simply not giving up on me. That shit is hot.

IT IS WHAT IT IS

At the root of much psychological distress is some form of non-acceptance or resistance of what is. People are generally stewing over the past or anticipating the future. Neither one usually leads to equanimity or peace of mind. In fact, both often lead to anxiety disorders, depression, compulsive and impulsive behavior, and laziness. Needless to say, non-acceptance and resistance will not motivate anyone to get in the game. What is the game? It's your life. It's your best life. It's the road to your best self. My colleague sat down with me this morning and staffed a case with me. Her online client suggested, "Maybe I just need to stay single the rest of my life." My colleague wasn't sure how to respond. I said, "Why does she need to figure this out?" It is what it is, and what will be, will be. If she bows out, she has made a choice. If she lives with and learns to tolerate the question and just "be," she won't feel compelled to jump into a bad relationship, resist offers, or define herself as any one particular thing. She'll remain open, hopeful, content, and at peace. That's the point. Not to figure out the past or control the future, which many people seek counseling for, but to learn to take life as it comes. This doesn't lead to inaction. On the contrary, it could lead to a whole new freedom and joy you've never known. It's a confident mentality of "I may not know, but I can learn or find out." Always embrace what is. Without judgment of how it "should" be. This leads to not getting out of bed. A "Why bother?" attitude. Get comfortable living with uncertainty. Then you will exude more confidence, experience more freedom, and get a start on your personal goals and growth.

HOW DO I START?

Now! According to a Chinese proverb, "The best time to plant a tree is twenty years ago; the second best time is today." Your life is now, not someday—not when you have all the answers and boxes checked. I used to smoke cigarettes, so quitting was always in the back of my mind, but it was never the "right" time. I used to think I'd quit when I graduated from high school, then it was college, then grad school, then when life got less stressful, or when my boyfriend quit. Then it was when I got married, then pregnant (it finally worked, but after how many years of damage?)—you get the idea. Pursue your goals now and don't put them off. Then stick to it despite what the voices around you and within you will say— basically anything to make you say fuck it. Keep your goals small and attainable and don't worry about what society says you haven't become yet. You may give up before you've begun. Society can be the biggest mirror for distorting your image into someone who is not good enough.

Some of the societal standards we try to measure ourselves up against are:

1.　Size two pants
2.　SAT score
3.　Golf score
4.　Body fat percentage
5.　Property size
6.　Clever conversation contributions
7.　Spouse attractiveness
8.　Talents
9.　Travels
10. Education

The list goes on and on. Some people won't bother with their goals because societal ideals are too far-reaching. Some people will go into hiding most of their lives because they don't feel as though they add up to some perfect standard. You don't owe anyone any of the above. You only owe yourself health, peace, and joy. Stop trying to keep up an image as if your worth rested on it. Jesus tells a man in the Bible that if he wants to be perfect, he must sell all his stuff, give the money to the poor, and follow Him (Matthew 19:21). He doesn't say to accumulate more, know more, be more, or do more. In fact, just the opposite… get your *worth* down to *nothing* and stop *aspiring* to being something great. Perfection is a product of having and wanting nothing. Unbecoming rather than becoming.

My youngest child fabricated a story about winning the spelling bee in her class last week. I did the usual high-five, "I'm so proud of you," display. My daughter has always struggled in school and needed tutors. When I found out she had lied, I panicked. She explained (screamed like a lunatic) to me that I'm never proud of her (insert eye roll here). Thinking back on how hard and for how long we pushed her to keep up with her classmates so that she would be accepted into private school with her sister was now haunting me. I wanted her to do well, but at what cost? Right or wrong, I felt compelled to say, "All right, it's time you heard this. I don't give a crap if you can spell. You're amazing. Don't lie to me again, or I won't be able to trust you." We must somehow separate our children's behaviors from their feelings of worth. But how? We must always speak to children about their behaviors and impress upon them that our love is unconditional. With any luck, they will grow into adults who are willing to make mistakes in front of others and accept their shortcomings without any loss of esteem.

Crystal was a nineteen-year-old client of mine who seemed to have been thrust into adulthood. She grew up in rural South Carolina with her dad. Her mom had left when she was eight, and she had no siblings. When she was eighteen, she married her teenage love. He joined the Marines, and before she knew it, she was in Hawaii, and he was deployed to Japan. She came to see me at her husband's prompting because she daily spent the better part of twenty-four hours in bed. It's not surprising that she began feeling depressed and anxious. Humans need a purpose, a sense of being part of something greater than themselves, of contributing to the good of the world, and of being seen and appreciated for their unique qualities. This doesn't happen in isolation. The Catch-22 is that isolation involves no mirrors. This is why involvement with society is risky for some: You can believe what is reflected back to you by society or have nothing reflected back and let your imagination assign your value apart from any outside input.

TO PEOPLE OR NOT TO PEOPLE

Peopling: the ability to tolerate people and their stupidity, as well as your own stupidity, in a public setting. To people, or engage in the act of peopling, is to be able to remain tactful despite a person's obvious stupidity and/or lack of social skills.

Introverts should not be confused with hiders. My friend Rich has chosen to enjoy a life of solitude in the Midwest. He has daily, but minimal, human contact in his community that he serves selflessly and joyfully. "I don't people much," he has explained to me. "No drama; I get to be me." And I'll admit I'd be hard-pressed to find a more jovial person than Rich. I believe what he means by "no drama" is that there are no competing forces telling him how one should function in the world, no anger at doing things differently than someone else, or judgment for how he chooses to live. He gets to just *be*. I've often wondered myself, *Who needs it?* As an extrovert, isolation makes me uneasy. I like having people-mirrors around. I'd rather be in a room full of strangers than in a room by myself. For the extrovert, life and purpose are clearer with other folks around, co-narrating life.

Only you can decide to what degree you are willing to participate in peopling. The temperament you were born with will compel you one way or another. But I believe, no matter how much or how little peopling you do, drama can be alleviated, if not extinguished, without moving to an unoccupied island in the middle of nowhere. In later chapters, we will discuss how to win people over and make friends (note: they are not the same thing)—every two years, on average, if you're a military spouse.

POLITICKING

Theresa came in for counseling following a neighborhood military spouses' Bunco game. For those of you who do not know, Bunco is a social dice game, involving 100 percent luck and no skill. It's not a super-intimate game since members of this Bunco club meet at least monthly and involve twelve or more players. Members take turns hosting, and it is a real opportunity to display your hospitality skills and even interior-decorating abilities. At the end of the night, Theresa left to return home feeling alone, misunderstood, and contending with the pangs of exclusion and inferiority. She explained that close conversations had gone on between peers that she was not involved in. They seemed to exude confidence and likeability, dominating conversations and laughing the night away. When I suggested some of them were extroverted and some were on a mission to impress, she responded, "That's just not me," in the most discouraged voice. "I wish I could be, and I'm mad at myself that I'm not. I was sick about it all weekend and avoided another function, and that only made me feel incompetent and isolated." We uncovered that Theresa was using this dog-and-pony show that we call Bunco as a measurement of her social standing, likeability, and hence, her value!

I have participated in several Bunco games. But for clarity, I sought out a definition to the word itself. What I discovered was most amusing.

Bunco: noun, 1. a swindle in which a person is cheated, persuaded to buy a worthless object, or otherwise victimized. 2. **Any misrepresentation**.

Wow. Don't get me wrong—I love a good Bunco game because I'm in it for the money and the yummy Pinterest dishes. But these types of functions…forced fun, mandatory fun…whatever you want to call them…are often like speed dating, sometimes popularity contests, and other times, an opportunity to kiss someone's ass. And I freaking love these women. They are motivated, enthusiastic, fit, determined, outgoing, patriotic, and supportive. I credit hanging around military spouses for making me sharper, more in shape, hospitable, independent, and supportive of my husband.

But…the environment is not one you should rate yourself against. The mirror can make you completely and utterly disgusted with yourself, especially if you're an introvert. Theresa needed to have some grace with herself for not loving or stealing the spotlight. She felt embarrassed by the attention she got on her wedding day! She's not a center-stage gal. She values close, intimate relationships, listening to others, and quietly sharing her experience and knowledge as a senior, or older Spouse. She has a lot to offer in social settings. But she was focused on what the setting said about her.

SHOW UP

Theresa wondered if she should continue to go to the Bunco games. "Gosh, I hope you do," I urged her. "You have so much to contribute, and the world is missing out when you retreat. You just can't go into these situations looking for *your place*. Go in looking for who you can put at ease or compliment. Ask yourself, 'What will I contribute tonight to someone else's comfort or good time'? It's likely there are gals there who also don't feel comfortable, miss their family back home, or would love to chat about their kids. Make it your mission to make someone feel liked and approved of, not to *be* liked and approved of. This is what leaders do. Oh, and by the way, the extroverts went home wondering whether they had been too obnoxious, had said something inappropriate, or had drank too much." (At least that's what I hear extroverts consider at the end of the night.) "Grab a caramel apple pie Jell-O shot and cracked-out cheddar bacon ranch turkey pinwheel, and get in the game!"

SUMMARY

I encourage you (the more modest folks of the world) to embrace your place in this world. I'd like you to find the courage to be unapologetically you, embracing all the nonsense. People-mirrors cannot always be avoided. We need to search ourselves for our judgments and perceptions that make peopling intolerable. Relationships force us to contend with our inner demons, so to speak. Sometimes you can control the number of relationships you participate in; sometimes you can't or simply don't want to. But make no mistake, relationships bring out your ugly eventually. And you will blame the person doing the reflecting for causing it. Banish people or banish inner demons. Both can be achieved at times. My friend Rich recently admitted that he is lonely. I feel for him. We are stuck in a world of wanting connections, mixed with a "mean people suck" reality. Sometimes people are legitimately mean, and sometimes we label them mean because they reflect a part of us we want to keep buried, or touch old wounds, or make us feel inadequate. Relationships can be fun and encouraging, but intimate relationships call you to be your highest self, not necessarily your most fun, best self. Your *self* that forces your sin to the surface so you can see it for what it is and grieve it, repent it, and receive forgiveness for it. And it sucks. It makes you long for holiness and purity—the things of the heavenly realm.

> "Love does not begin and end
> the way we seem to think it does.
> Love is a battle
> Love is a war
> Love is growing up."
>
> — James A. Baldwin

EXERCISE

1. What promises, vows, and commitments have you made in your life and to whom?

   _____

   _____

   _____

   _____

2. List five traits that annoy you and that you judge others for (fake boobs, an obnoxious laugh, or being lazy, overweight, or always late).

   _____

   _____

   _____

3. In what ways do you try to impress others (story told, languages spoken, muscles on top of muscles)?

    _____

    _____

    _____

    _____

4. Who in your life cannot be avoided? How does that person make you feel about yourself?

    _____

    _____

    _____

    _____

5. Finish this sentence: I wish I were more like _____.

Chapter 4

Genu-Winning

"No one can make you feel inferior without your consent."

— Eleanor Roosevelt

In the last chapter, I spoke about people reflecting a side of you that you don't like. Generally, this happens because you feel the person makes you misrepresent yourself. Once you do open up, you risk becoming a target of theirs and others' judgments. When that doesn't line up with the *image* you are trying to create for yourself, you may end up resenting that person, begin to banish people from your life, judge others, grow defensive, or descend into self-doubt. To be genuine and unmasked without defenses and shame is to truly win at doing you. That's when genu-winning happens.

TRANSPARENCY

Have you ever met someone who seems so transparent that they do not appear to be performing at all? I have a few friends like that on Facebook, where I find myself at times operating with my defense mechanisms. They are not ashamed to tell you the good, bad, and ugly of their lives. They don't pretend to be perfect or have perfect lives. They are not always impressive, but when they are, you can be certain their next Facebook post will be way less glamorous. I envy that transparency. People who talk freely about their marriage's imperfections or how their weight loss left them with sagging skin that they hide well are refreshingly genuine. You just get that they are not trying to live up to something. They are *real*. And why not? Really. *Why not?* My guess is that a lot of us are competing and keeping score—serving the ego; that is, our image.

"FEEL MY MUSCLE"

I was raised a competitor. I was raised a winner. I believe much of my image was formulated on coming out on top, being the best. This was extremely helpful for a girl who would otherwise feel inferior to her peers. My dad was crazy-empowering as my softball coach, but my ego development involved being "better than" the competition. That's how I managed my fragile self-esteem—by finding someone to measure myself against and be better. This was simple, easy, exhausting, and, of course, not real. I suspect a lot of people fall somewhere on the spectrum of comparison. On the high end, you have a range of narcissism, from "full-blown" to "exhibiting traits." These folks are all about their own image. Entirely. They are great; you are not. They size up others on Facebook, perhaps feeling better or worse about themselves afterward. They only post the "good" pictures. They search for someone in the gym who is worse off than them. They brag about their credit score/body fat percentage/the thick-ass book they read/how much their car cost/ sexual conquests/kids activities/travels/who their friends are. They feel their best when they've been complimented. They avoid conflict. Perhaps even you can relate? But somewhere in the middle, you have average folks, like you and me, who are tempted or wired or groomed to portray one or two of these characteristics.

IMPRESSION MANAGEMENT

Doormats — People-Pleasers — Impressers — Intimidators — Bullies — Narcissists

I designed this spectrum to illustrate the shortcuts we often take to gain feelings of self-worth. It is always at your own or another's expense. It comes with a price tag. The more in the middle we are, the less extreme our behavior and the more likely these traits will go unnoticed as our cover for lack of self-worth. I encourage you to take an honest look at yourself here. Many normal, successful, likeable people are, or once were, on this spectrum. Some have evolved to function more truly, more genuinely; some go back and forth depending on mood, lack of sleep, uncertainty, transitions, or desperate moments of feeling like a nobody. We all experience these times, particularly if we're starting out or starting over. It's about creating our image. Social media has made this even more irresistible. We've never been more on-stage than we are right now. People are watching and judging, and our image seems much more important than it really is.

I was bullied by a boy in junior high who, I believe, exerted his dominance over me to feel better about himself. When I got older, I would fantasize about putting Sheldon in his place. He put me down, and for years, I conjured up this scenario in my mind where I would put him down harder and even more publicly. I believe his bullying drastically affected my self-image. He targeted me, which meant I was different. The other girls were left alone. It had to be just me—something about me. I wasn't measuring up. I would search others' appearances for answers and do anything just to blend in. No, I would outshine. Instead of becoming a doormat or a bully myself, I became impressive. For you parents out there, I believe my involvement in sports and affirmations from my dad made the difference. I've always had my eye on self-improvement and maintaining the empowering messages I received at home on the field. But too much of anything is unhealthy, as we will see. Below, we will take a closer look at the impresser, doormat, and bully. The narcissists aren't reading this book, so I won't bother with them.

IMPRESSER

The impresser puts being impressive above being loved. Sure they appear to (and may even do) have a charmed life. But they worked hard for it. And to what end? Being desired, envied, and emulated over simple things—simple pleasures, simple moments, simple sweetness. These folks may miss opportunities to really connect to people because they are focused on maintaining a winning image. Not really happy in the shadows/unknown, this person often steals the spotlight, is up for anything adventurous and fun, and has a lot of friends as long as they are not too intimidating (people are generally drawn to others who make them comfortable, not intimidated). This person isn't entirely genuine. They want to be liked and like what they see in the mirror. They are usually quite impressive, but once this person is exposed as flawed or mediocre in relationship to others, the obsession to prevail can be costly. For me, the cost was related to my mothering and marriage. I would resist hugs if my hair was done, lose my cool if the children spilled something on my clean floor, hate myself for hating breastfeeding, or accuse my husband of wanting someone better.

My aunt Cindy is teaching me to evolve from this, but she doesn't know it. I simply watch her extend herself for others without a care in the world for whom she is impressing or whether she is adored. Why? Because life to her is about everything you will wish you had done on your deathbed: traveled to see loved ones, baked cookies with your nieces and nephews, lost a few hours of sleep to help a family member, missed the gym to take a friend to the doctor, skipped a cleaning day to take your kids to the park, sacrificed your tan to do cannonballs with your kids, put down your self-betterment book to get buried in the sand, or worn last season's styles just because you didn't give an eff. At the end of your life, do you want to have been loved or impressive?

DOORMAT/PEOPLE-PLEASER

These two are different degrees of the same type of image-manager. It is likely that more people relate to people-pleaser, as doormat is extreme. Most people have some boundaries for what they are willing to do and how they are willing to be treated. Extreme doormats, however, accept mean and egregious behavior, which, in turn, lets people know how they may treat them. People-pleasers don't necessarily tolerate this sort of ugliness, but saying no is hard for them. They seek the favor of friends and family by trying to make everyone happy. They try to obtain outside approval by setting their own wants or needs aside. Just like the bully and impresser, they lack their own internal yardstick to measure value, so they seek out validation from others via their approval. This comes in the form of doing favors, going above and beyond, going along with the group, or accepting others' questionable ideas. This causes the pleaser to betray their own values, good judgment, self-respect, personal time and space, and rest.

My friend Sierra grew up with a dad who had severe PTSD from the Vietnam War. Similar to having an alcoholic or controlling parent, keeping him happy was an act of survival. Children who endure this environment may become adults whose identity as a pleaser is based on their skill for being helpful, cheerful, selfless, and capable. It's no surprise that they can be taken advantage of, used, and tossed when they're of no more use. Again, if this describes you, I want to help you evolve, not change. Please don't stop being generous and loving. Our world needs more of your kind—but be kind to yourself as well.

INTIMIDATOR/BULLY

Our world needs bullies and/or intimidators…to shut the hell up and be kinder to others. I've been told by the people who know me best (my family and best friends), that I'm bossy, pushy, direct, and intimidating. Their words, not mine. Not one for exchanging pleasantries or meaningless small talk, I am often short and to the point—probably even rude at times. To me, I am assertive. I hope that's how others see it too. In Chapter 10, we'll take a closer look at assertiveness, making yourself clear, and asking for what you need while respecting other people's rights to polite and courteous treatment. For now, let's look at the all-out bully.

Think bullying doesn't happen in your circle? Think you're never the culprit? Let's do a litmus test of the more covert and common form of grown-ass-adult-people-bullying. These people take others down subtly. They joke at another person's expense, use sarcasm, condescending body language (looks, gestures), deliberately cause embarrassment, and use social or professional exclusion. Where's the safest place to convey these messages? From behind a computer screen. They are one-way mirrors: I get to see you, but you don't get to see me. Once again, social media provides a platform to boldly and bravely put others down in an attempt to build themselves up.

I had a grown-up bully in my life. Like most, bullies appear appropriate on the outside. But if your senses are keen, you can easily recognize their take-down moves on social media, the ones that have many people wondering, *Are they talking about me?* Sometimes you will know they are. Posts that relate exactly to what you were talking about and how the person now perceives you will come moments after a texting conversation. In my case, it was I "take things too personally," followed by a vaguely targeted Facebook meme about how "People who take things personally should fall over like a goat." Something like that. This followed a conversation where I privately texted her, asking her to stop airing her grievances on social media, as we were role models for other young, impressionable spouses. What I remember most clearly about that post was all the comments that followed from her friends about how ridiculous and laughable and high school some people (me) are. This went on for days between her and her friends (who had never met me), never acknowledging whom they were talking about, but with me knowing damn well. It hurt. But I guess that was the point. I know *intellectually* that her behavior speaks more about her than about me. But I withdrew completely from this person because I let her get to me. I wasn't aware and in control of my triggers enough to deal with her, so I fled.

EVOLUTION

Now that we can identify some of the shortcuts to false self-esteem, let's decide today to grow up. In my mind, growing up or evolving looks like this:

People-pleasers become people-considerers.

Impressers become influencers.

Intimidators become asserters.

Bullies become humble.

People-pleasers can be more genuine when they are helping, participating, or accommodating from a place of fullness of their own needs. They can consider other people's needs and desires after they are firmly rooted in their own value system and rested. They can confidently say no to things that would overexert, betray these values, or come from a desire to be liked or acceptable.

Impressers can be more genuine when they strive to better themselves without losing moments of dirty, messy love. They can step outside of themselves to promote another's wellbeing and happiness at the sacrifice of selfish gains and desires. They can sit through annoying cartoons, pass by mirrors without checking, be and not *do* for a season of life, and order the cheesecake. They inspire others with their zest for life and encouraging words, not by being *better than*.

Bullies can be more genuine when they speak up against outrageous behavior or abuse and for tolerance and fairness without being meaner than the injustice. They also don't create more injustice in the process. They don't squash another person to make their point. They give imagined adversaries the benefit of the doubt before speaking out with slanderous words. They are open to being wrong, can withstand correction because they know that they, too, are not perfect, and know they have a lot to learn in this lifetime.

SUMMARY

> "Childhood is what you spend the rest of
> your life trying to overcome."
>
> — Birdee Pruitt, *Hope Floats*

We are all in recovery. We got so many mixed messages throughout our childhood and adolescence about who we are and whom we should be that it was inevitable we would cling to at least one of them. The idea of self-growth is to evolve to the next spectrum, not overcompensate by moving toward the opposite extreme. That's just another cover up. Do you want to be more genuine? Are you tired of wearing a mask or a letter on your chest, or are you afraid you'll be figured out? Do you want more harmony? Rest? Authenticity? If you've been eaten up and spit out by others at a young age, chances are you formed a place in your mind where it was you against the world. Kill or be killed. Be liked or suffer. I hope you take on the challenge to be more genuine because it's a relief for everyone involved when you are real, humble, and flawed. To me, that contributes to making our world a better place.

EXERCISE

1. Can you relate to any of these areas of functioning? If so, which ones and in which settings or specific relationships?

   _____

   _____

   _____

   _____

2. What would it mean for you to evolve into a more genuinely functioning person?

   _____

   _____

   _____

   _____

3. How can you make being relatable instead of being liked a priority?

   _____

   _____

   _____

Chapter 5

Building Confidence

"It takes courage to grow up and become who you really are."

— e. e. cummings

UNF*CK YOURSELF

This is an expression often heard in military culture. It typically means: Search yourself, get your head on straight, and change course. When I asked my husband what he would do if I ever confessed to him that I was having an affair, he said, "I'd tell you to un-fuck yourself." He would expect me to figure out the disillusionment that led to the affair and do the right thing. I love his confidence in me! I love Service Members for this mentality. I sometimes use this term with regard to recovering from all forms of blinded-ness we experience as human beings in a fallen world. Blinded-ness is the opposite of wisdom (how God sees things). How do we begin to open our eyes? Try for a minute to remember who you were before all that bad shit happened. Before the world told you that you were wrong—not good enough. Before that person told you there was someone better or you don't count, or you aren't special/invited/wanted/needed the way you are. Maybe it was a traumatic event that occurred long ago. One or more of these things have happened to every single one of us at some point. That person you were before is your authentic self, the one you were created to be. The one who spreads mercy and peace because that is what springs from the un-effed version of yourself. That person. Maybe some people, or one person, gets to see that self. If you're lucky, that person is your significant other. With this person, you have no pretenses. You can be vulnerable. They know you intimately, flaws and all, and love you just the way you are. We get back to that person by healing, not drinking, or lifting, or hustling, or showering—but by healing.

WHO, WHAT, WHERE, WHEN, HOW?

Do you have a picture in your mind yet of that person, the one you were before you weren't enough? The person we weren't trying to be because our family wanted us to be that person. For me, it's the dirty-faced eight-year-old who didn't care that she looked like a boy, played "guns," held worms, brought home dead birds, and was just *wild*. I don't remember wondering if God loved me or if I was good enough. It must be what Adam and Eve felt like before they realized they were naked. Imagine just being, unaware, unashamed, and you suddenly get the knowledge that you are wrong and unpleasing. In Genesis 3, God asked Adam and Eve, "Who told you you were naked? Have you eaten from the tree that I commanded you not to eat from?" This was a pivotal and devastating moment for humankind. After it, we were forever plunged into the abyss of *feeling* shame and condemnation.

How sad is that? This was not God's plan for us. I can almost imagine the sadness God must have felt knowing we had been deceived and would feel forever deprived. God clothed Adam and Eve and kicked them out of the garden. The entire story points to God's love for us. The rule was meant to keep us safe, happy, and blissfully unaware. The rule was broken, and God reconciled us by clothing us. Then God gave us reprieve from living in a place where we would never die and live eternally in this despair. So, here we are now. Out of the garden, feeling condemned every day. We have the gift of being clothed in the blood of Jesus and a death that will break us free and send us back into eternal bliss. Should we choose to accept it.

But if you're reading this, then you're still alive and contending with these feelings. It's human nature. It's almost automatic. We cling to Scripture and worship as a way to try to bring on the feeling of unconditional, crazy love for just being ourselves, but our flesh is convinced we must *earn* any sort of favor. It's a daily battle between being filled with Spirit or filled with ego.

SPIRIT VS. EGO

Whether your peace of mind comes from being one with nature, one with God, or one with the universe, the day-to-day reality is a feeling of separateness. The mind is littered with thoughts of judgment, expectations, and labels. The world becomes our mirror, reflecting back to us a less-than image. Peers become measuring sticks; we strive to be greater; we work for our parents' approval; we are just trying desperately to be acceptable—good enough. This inauthentic self is the ego. The authentic self is filled with Spirit. Spirit is whatever you connect to that is the source of freely given love, purity, and holiness. For me, that is the Lord, my Creator. When this connection is made, whether through hiking, meditating, or worshipping, you feel more "right," more confident. Your cup over-floweth.

But comparison awaits. Inevitably, the standard of worth will shift back to what is physically right in front of you. Someone better, someone with traits you long for, someone whom you disappoint, someone whom you, yourself, judge. This is the kind of information that the ego thrives on. The ego is your *story*. It's who you were, are, and will be. It's based on the accumulation of your accomplishments, aspirations, and failures. In contrast, the spirit of you is connected, immeasurable, and indestructible. Some call this *enlightenment*. Buddha defines this term as the end of suffering. I don't think ego and enlightenment coexist. I think your story actually perpetuates pain and suffering, not peace. It's called an existential *crisis* for a reason. There's nothing peaceful or fun about it. It's the moment when an individual questions whether their life has meaning, purpose, or value. It can result in or from major depressive disorder, obsessive-compulsive disorder, alcohol use disorder, prolonged isolation, dissatisfaction with one's life, and more. It's based on introspection, comparison, a tally of life's accomplishments, a question of why any of it matters, and a desire to *define* life based on choices made—or not made. Just thinking about it makes me start to panic. But this is life outside the garden. We are condemned to freedom.

WHAT'S YOUR STORY?

As a therapist, there's not much I love more than hearing a person's story and then highlighting the pivotal moments and times of bravery in it, in hopes of changing the way the person chooses to tell their story. One of my favorite stories was portrayed in a movie called *Straight Outta Compton*. To me, this film is a story of magnificent talent in a severely disadvantaged setting, where stars aligned to make underprivileged lyrical and vocal geniuses a huge success. Yes, a lot of carnage and debauchery occurred as this true tale unfolded, but I'm a sucker for a good something-outta-nothing story.

Who isn't? I love the grit involved, the hope for us all! Most self-help and empowerment books and counseling aim to help make your story a fabulous one. The ego depends on this information to thrive and feel good about itself. If we get our stories right, we can feel okay about ourselves. All stories have a beginning, middle, and end. We search all areas at different times, connecting the dots to make sense of why we are who we are and how to get to where we are going. Needless to say, most folks come into counseling with the past or the future in mind. They can't get over something that already happened, or they are anticipating something that hasn't yet happened. The anxiety about this stems from the thought that their identification of self depends on reconciling it.

"Do you have a problem *right now,* as in, in this moment?" Clients typically look at me sideways when I ask them this question. They often respond, "I just told you all my problems, so yes, I do." Then we problem-solve what we can, create a plan for anticipated troubles, and do a bit of grieving for the past. Many people walk around all day as if they have a problem right now. Once we've talked, I ask the question again, and they start to get it. "No, I don't have a problem in this particular moment, at this time, in this room." Then I encourage them to ask themselves that question routinely throughout the day when they are feeling anxious or angry. Almost always the answer will be no. Try it for yourself!

"Problems" generally exist in the mind's time continuum. Exceptions include having to use the toilet on the highway with no exits in sight, being in the midst of battle, and needing to break away from a conversation when the other person won't stop talking. All other "problems" are usually related to anticipation of an event, situation, or conversation or ruminating on something that was done or said twenty years ago…or yesterday—it's still the past. If you don't have a problem "right now," go back to paying attention to what is physically right in front of you. Your life!

CONSCIOUS VS. UNCONSCIOUS LIVING

How do you pay attention to what is right in front of you? Easy. Put down your phone and use your senses to get in touch with your physical world and get out of your head. Smell the air, feel the ground under your feet, notice your surroundings, taste your food with all of your attention. If you are in bed doing nothing and trying to sleep, put your hand on your stomach and count to four on the inhale and then again on the exhale and feel your belly rise and fall. This is paying attention to the now. If you are in a meeting and your mind starts to wander, pull yourself back to the present by noticing how the chair you are sitting in feels, its texture, padding. You are retraining your mind to come back to the moment. This will become effortless over time. The things that will make returning to the moment much harder to achieve are *drinking* and *downtime*. The good news is you can control your time spent doing either. You have more power over your problems than you may be allowing yourself to believe.

A more peaceful existence relies on being in the *now* at all times. You need only ask yourself the simple question, "Do I have a problem right now?" throughout the day to bring your awareness back into the current moment. All else has either passed or can't yet be dealt with. When my daughter was eight years old, I explained to her that one day she would go off to college and live on her own. She insisted that I agree to move in with her. At the time, her current self could not get comfortable with the notion that her future self would be just fine going off alone. The thought made her very anxious, and I couldn't explain to her my plan to help her grow up first—that by the time she was a teenager, she would be ready and willing to go off on her own without me. Her eight-year-old self wasn't buying it. This is what we do when we are anxious about the future. Our present self can't wrap our mind around what we have coming up. We forget that God plans to help us grow up first. We *will* be ready in that moment, not a day before.

People often base their true selves on what they have done or what has happened to them in the past. This also causes anxiety. Sometimes they believe what they will accomplish, or not, is the determining factor. The authentic self is not based on these principles. It's based in who you are the day you were born. A beautiful creation, not a bastard-child, not a heroin baby, not an orphan, not an inbred. Those are all stories created from people's choices, labels, or judgments. You just *are*, no matter how you got here or how anyone feels about you being here. And that is unshakeable. God's promises are yours to claim as well.

Still having trouble feeling your worth and value? The most concrete steps I can offer you are to stay in the present moment as much as possible. When you drift to the past or future, pull yourself back with curiosity, not judgment. Notice traits and ambitions you have taken on in a nonjudgmental way. They just are. We are playing a game, and our ego is *loving* it. Just recognize when this is happening, and don't let that false sense of self rob you of your happiness and peace of mind. Ultimately, none of us are the products of our stories. We take nothing with us in the end but the love we generated. Know that others are normally reacting to their own egos and perhaps you will be less judgmental yourself. It's a freeing truth and piece of wisdom. Don't be blinded by what your ego needs to survive or be so harsh with others about what their egos need—compliments, validation, victory, accolades, spotlights, laughs, attention, or whatever. People crave these things. Forgive them; it's not personal. The ego isn't going *anywhere* until physical death occurs.

AUTHENTIC RELATIONSHIPS

True confidence has no competition. It is not a result of beating, winning, excelling, or advancing. That is false confidence, which requires a competitor and is situationally dependent. You become as confident as you are able to become by being *better than* your competitor. This is just a construct of the ego. As a competitive athlete most of my childhood, it has been a difficult construct for me to shake. One of my favorite attributes in a person is quiet confidence. It's not loud or haughty. It's not boasting. It's a person who knows their worth despite their reflection in the mirrors all around them. I used to go confidently into situations because I convinced myself I was the best one there. I *exuded* self-assuredness. It's an easy way to carry yourself, and it came naturally to me, but it was shaky. Some days, I didn't care what anyone thought; some days, I did. I didn't take criticism well. I didn't take a lot of feedback well. It certainly made my marriage uncomfortable. I cared what this man thought of me *a lot*. The problem was that it all had to be good, or he had defects in his perception.

True confidence is quiet. It doesn't exude anything. It doesn't demand *likes* or validation. It *does* care what others think, and adjusts if need be for the health of a functional team. It's the ability to be authentic. It's not shaken. The receptionist at my children's school is truly authentic. She just seems to be rooted in the knowledge that she is loved, accepted, and valued. She's not looking around for these things or defending herself to others. She seems unaware of herself. Not that she doesn't keep herself up; she's just focused on serving others and making others feel okay and understood, which is not easy when she is the first line of defense for frustrated and scattered parents (okay, me). She has nothing to stand up for, defend, or announce with her stature. She's just lovely, as if her cup is overflowing. You could trust her with all your secrets, and she wouldn't judge you. Now, imagine a relationship where two people like this can be transparent with one another and not worry about judgment or disapproval. They are able to give and receive information about one another without any threat of withholding affection or love. They use no manipulative ninja moves to gain the other's approval. The benefit of an authentic relationship is longevity. Do you think you could grow old and fat with someone you don't believe unconditionally loves the authentic, genuine you? There's a lot less anger and defensiveness in this relationship. Angry and defensive people are avoided or appeased, understandably, even by their spouse. It is an exceptional individual who seeks authenticity. The competitive spirit of our culture promotes winning (thank you, Charlie Sheen), not sincerity.

SUMMARY

One of the greatest challenges in life is being yourself in a world that's trying to make you like everyone else. Many people get their esteem from their story, other people, or being in their element. Take any person and put them in an uncomfortable situation, put them in a relationship, or introduce a change or transition into their life and you'll see someone calling up a therapist (hopefully). Although I love the job security, I don't aim to make more money by prolonging the problem. Chances are the ego is struggling to maintain its image and self-worth in a setting you don't shine in, a relationship that exposes your flaws, or a transition that makes you unsure of yourself. Confidence is shaken. So, are you going to impress? Maybe bully? Maybe charm people into liking you? What if you can't? What if you disappoint? What if you're simply not liked? Gasp!

EXERCISE

1. What criticism would you find most difficult to look at honestly?

   _____

   _____

   _____

   _____

2. With whom do you struggle to be authentic?

   _____

   _____

   _____

   _____

3. What obstacles keep you from being your true self?

   _____

   _____

   _____

   _____

4. With whom do you find it easy to be your true self?

   _____

   _____

   _____

   _____

5. What achievements and accomplishments do you find yourself talking about the most?

    _____

    _____

    _____

    _____

Chapter 6

Banning Shame

"Make peace with your pieces."

— r.h. Sin

I read a sentiment online today that said, "Today, in science class, I learned every cell in our entire body is replaced every seven years. How lovely it is to know one day I will have a body that you will have never touched." I thought how healing this idea could be at the end of a breakup or other offensive encounter. We are physically unbecoming throughout life and growing and evolving in new ways. Literally!

Shame is not being *able* to unbecome your perceived identity. It's carrying around an idea of who you were and always will be. Sometimes, like after a trauma, it's about who you were and will never get to be again. Shame stops you from taking risks, claiming things you deserve, having peace of mind, and evolving into a new or different self. In the previous chapters, we examined the potential gap that lies between who you are, who you were, and who you are meant to be. Relationships challenge us to bridge those gaps, go into hiding, or live a life of trickery and inauthenticity. In this chapter, we'll look our accuser squarely in the face and, hopefully, make a *decision* to be unashamedly us, with all we've experienced, receiving the unconditional love we are entitled to, not what we think we deserve.

DECISIONS, DECISIONS

I say "decision" because I believe a lot of our healthy emotional responses are just that—a decision. Love is a choice I try to make on a daily basis despite my mood, energy level, or desire. I know I have great people in my life, and it is selfish to expect them to meet my needs without loving them in return. It's also part of the plan to love without receiving in return. It's our obligation in this world to spread love. It's the second of the two most important commandments in Christianity, and whatever your religion, I hope it's deemed important. Some choices I make even when I don't feel like it are:

1. Reading to my children
2. Cooking for my husband
3. Staying in shape for my family
4. Putting extra effort into a potluck dish
5. Sharing food from my plate at a restaurant
6. Complimenting people

Just the same, ridding yourself of shame is a decision. Shaming voices in your head are typically recordings of people from your past, evil whispering doubt in your ear, or some form of self-inflicted punishment. Maybe someone from your past has squashed your self-worth out of their own self-hatred or in a cheap attempt to build their own self-esteem. That voice was recorded in your psyche and now replays in social situations. One of Satan's tactics to steal our joy and peace is to demoralize us and make us question our abilities and places in this world. Satan's tactic for bullies, on the other hand, is to create a false sense of dominance, entitlement, and arrogance, causing disputes, hurt feelings, and shame. These recordings and Satan's antagonizing occur often when we are in the company of others. Social situations, big or small, are ripe with opportunities for comparison, judging, and self-loathing. Just like love is a choice, banning your internal shame is a choice. Some tempting, quick-fixes for alleviating or banning feelings of shame are:

1. Drinking, drugging, or any numbing behavior
2. Cutting people out of our lives, going into hiding, and hurting the person who brings about those feelings
3. Shaming others before they have the opportunity to shame us

We do these things because we don't know any better and because shame sucks. People *kill* themselves because they hate themselves and feel ashamed, like they are a burden, unworthy, and hopeless.

IDENTIFYING IT

This morning I stepped on a scale for the first time in about a year. I stopped weighing myself because I didn't like how attached I got to the number, and having built a bit of muscle over the past ten years, it doesn't behoove me to know that number any more. I always step off the scale in astonishment at my weight, and I then think way too much about it afterward. I once got to the gym, weighed myself, and left without ever exercising. It was a "fuck this—what's the point" moment. I admire my husband's ability to keep track of his weight daily, even weighing himself at the end of the day, after supper, with clothes on! His sense of self is completely unrelated to his body weight, but he does like to stay aware of it so he can manage to stay within military standards. Lately, however, I've been feeling *guilty* for the overeating I've been doing. It's starting to take shape—in my ass and thighs.

Anyhow, my coworker and good friend, Raul, has been trying to gain weight, so we agreed to a little friendly competition, trying to get to each other's weight. He would like to be closer to mine; I would like to be closer to his. So, we agreed to a twelve-week challenge, and whoever comes the closest wins. To be fair, we both stepped on the scale to get an accurate count of how many pounds we'd have to burn or gain. I was *embarrassed* at how much the previous few months of gluttonous behavior had stuck around to taunt me. I was within two pounds of my highest (non-pregnancy) weight ever. I can say this because I'm not ashamed—I'm embarrassed, but empowered to change. Nor do I think weight makes a person a moron or a loser. I felt guilty about my recent binging behavior. I had decreased the Prozac I take for my horrid PMS, thinking, *I live in Hawaii. Surely, I can make myself happy*," which I believe was somewhat responsible for the multiple bags of brownie brittle I had bought, the box of wine emptying much sooner than usual, and plates of nachos disappearing into my own face. I knew this was unnecessary behavior, and I was *annoyed* at myself for basically ruining all my hard work in the gym. But I didn't hate, nor condemn myself. I chose to treat myself with grace and mercy and embrace the hope that exists in getting back on track.

TACKLING IT

Guilt. Embarrassment. Annoyance at self. These are all feelings that wake us up to the fact that we are living outside of the parameters of the road toward our best selves. These feelings are normal and appropriate and meant to motivate us back into the realm of growth and betterment. They are uncomfortable, sure, but imagine the person who refuses to ever experience them. They are either a recluse, avoiding all contact with mankind, or a narcissist.

Shame, however, paralyzes. It causes hopelessness, self-loathing, numbing behaviors, laziness, and isolation. I have a dear friend I'll call Lynn, who struggles with feelings of shame. She is overly-apologetic for simple mistakes or even things that were no one's fault. One day, we were talking about her fear of dentists. She wanted a referral for a kind and gentle professional. Later in the conversation, she was reduced to tears when she told me she had a secret and, besides her husband, she had never told a soul. "I am so embarrassed and ashamed," she said. The way she was building up to the horrifying truth she was about to tell, I thought she might never tell me. She finally pulled out her bridge, which replaced two molars she had pulled years earlier. She took it right out of her mouth and said, "Look!", holding it close to my face. I examined the bridge for a few moments, and then said, "I don't see it. What am I looking for?" "The bridge!" her eyes filled with tears. "I don't understand," I offered. And I truly didn't. I could not for the life of me figure out what she was so upset about. She stuck it back in her mouth and said, "I can't believe I told you that. I have never told anyone I have that."

Lynn struggles with bouts of seclusion and numbing behavior (alcohol, in her case). I can see why. She is denying parts of her existence out of pure shame, and for what? This woman would give anyone the shirt off her back in the middle of a blizzard, and yet she feels like an embarrassment most of the time. I adore her, and the world is missing out when she goes into hiding. It angers me to think about whoever created and/or upholds these feelings of shame in her. All I know is that I hope she believes me when I tell her, "You are wonderful the way you are and should hide nothing. You have nothing to feel bad about." Of all things, dental work! I went on to share my story about the hair transplant I had received ten years earlier. She gasped, especially when I told her, "I've told a lot of people."

BANNING IT

I'm not gonna lie. I wrote the previous chapter yesterday, and then lay in bed last night contemplating all this self-disclosure. The acne, the balding, the bossiness. Not to mention, I am a horrible example of a Christian. Good Lord, I might as well divulge how many sexual partners I've had. I wondered if all this cringe-worthy transparency was really necessary and whether it would make me more credible and respectable. I can't sell shamelessness to you in this book while lying to you. I struggled with my thoughts last night. I almost re-wrote the whole chapter on shame because of shame. How poignant.

As I grappled with my insecurities regarding fully disclosing my most embarrassing traits, decisions, and mistakes, I was forced to reconsider my thoughts about the subject. I adore people who are transparent, want to give others permission to be unashamed-ly themselves, and love good, self-deprecating humor. But now I'm faced with the issue of *hypocrisy*, or pretense. Hypocrisy, from the Greek word *hypokritai*, means "stage acting." It's not a genuine por-trayal of oneself, but the transformation of one's self to win another's laughter or affection. The audience demands entertainment, and the hypocrite says or does whatever is pleasing to that crowd, despite core beliefs. This may be one thing to one crowd and the opposite to another. The tugs urging me back into approval and applause are powerful. I want to impress you, gain your admiration, and hell, even adoration. But at what price?

When I am acting like a hypocrite and pretending to be someone I'm not, I believe I am disconnecting from my Lord, the One who created me, sustains me, and provides for me. That is a high price to pay. I am now connected to and focused on the world's standard and idea of me. This will cost me joy, peace, and sanity, to name just a few of the costs.

Matthew 6:24 says: "No one can serve two masters. Either you will hate the one and love the other, or you will be devoted to the one and despise the other. You cannot serve both God and money."

Money is one example. You also cannot serve both God and the admiration of others. This is why God asks us to worship and tithe in secret and rewards us for that.

Matthew 6:4: "So that your giving may be *in secret*. Then your Father, who sees *what is done in secret*, will reward you." [Emphasis mine.]

Matthew 6:6: But when you pray, go into your room, close the door and pray to your Father, who is unseen. Then your Father, who sees what is done in secret, will reward you.

Matthew 6:18: So that it will not be obvious to others that you are fasting, but only to your Father, who is unseen; and your Father, who sees *what is done in secret*, will reward you.

When we pray or do our good deeds in secret, it shows we place more value on what *only* God sees you do than any single person on this earth. It means you know God, and you know God *sees you*. You are connected intimately. God is not just a distant, strange authority running the universe. You know your true value to God and make the Lord your priority.

Satan hates you. Remember that. The Evil One doesn't want you to feel loved or valuable or liked or worthy. Lucifer wants you to go into hiding or boost yourself up so that others go into hiding. It was the first thing Adam and Eve did following an encounter with Satan. Out of shame, they hid, presuming God would be displeased and angry with them. Yet God did the most loving thing— clothed them and saved them from an eternal existence of shame and despair. That's why our final clothing in the blood of Christ is important to claim. Not only can you let go of past shame, but you will be let off the hook for your current limitations too.

EMBRACING THE GIFT

Jennifer was a client who had recently become a Christian and wanted to discuss the immense divide she felt there was between her and God. She had been examining Scripture closely, trying to figure out and reconcile what seemed like opposing verses. Everything seemed to point to her guilt, and she was feeling condemned. Everywhere she looked, she found her flaws, failures, and lack of salvation. She would read something loving and merciful, but even that made her feel undeserving and horrible about herself. That is the misfortune of living in this fallen world and sinful flesh. She couldn't accept a free gift without having earned it, deserved it, or at least living up to the purity and holiness that God calls us to. She was barricaded in shame with her shortcomings, despite knowing she had God's forgiveness the moment she asked.

The truth is you aren't perfect, and God's eye is on perfecting Creation. But even when we take small steps in faith, God is proud. Even if we think we should have done better sooner. George MacDonald said, "God is easy to please, but hard to satisfy." C. S. Lewis compares God's love to a parent teaching their child to walk. The parent is most pleased with the child's first feeble attempt at walking, even when the child ultimately falls short of the goal by stumbling and knocking shit over (my words, not Lewis'). The parent may even take pictures or video or applaud. But no parent will settle for this toddling ability; they will encourage the child to keep going and to try again until they are walking tall and strong like the adult they are growing up to be.

There's no shame in falling short. Jennifer wasn't claiming the grace, mercy, and freedom that Jesus had died to give her. I suggested that she was in a mourning period. Grieving your sinful nature is part of the journey. The more you get to know God, and rely on God's holiness and purity, the worse you tend to feel about yourself. You begin to recognize how despicable your nature truly is. A sheep looks pretty white in a green pasture—until it snows.

When we get to know Jesus, we are sheep in the snow, wondering how we went from looking so good to looking so dirty. Maybe people feel pretty good about themselves, ya know, compared to Osama Bin Laden. But compared to Jesus, we are pretty yucky. So, yeah, shame, doubt, and grief may ensue, but you aren't meant to stay there. This is one part of your journey. After you realize and grieve your icky-ness, you will be amazed that Jesus died for you. I hope you accept this free gift.

No, you don't deserve it. No, you can't earn it. No, you can't pay it back. All glory to God.

SUMMARY

The first person Jesus revealed himself to as the Messiah was a woman of questionable morals (John 4:42). He knew her life; she felt unworthy even to be talking to him; he gave her hope and the truth she was looking for, and she went on to tell many people about him. These people also went on to believe he was the Messiah. Our walk is a wee bit longer, but that's it in a nutshell. Maybe you can't tell just anyone about your messes, but you can tell your Creator. You can find a therapist or a trusted friend whom you know can handle your emotions without judgment or criticism. Unfortunately, not everyone can be trusted with your secrets. I trust you, dear reader, to have some leniency with my confessions. Decide today to put your issues out there to someone as a first step in owning them and accepting them as a part of your journey. Know that your shortcomings do not define who you are. Then get out of yourself, and go love someone else because you are off the hook, not on it.

EXERCISE

1. What are some ways you can choose to love others today?

   _____

   _____

   _____

   _____

2. What makes you feel shame and how do you cope with those feelings?

   _____

   _____

   _____

   _____

3. In what ways are you a hypocrite? Whom do you aim to please and why?

   _____

   _____

   _____

   _____

4. What is your most shameful truth? Write it out here. What would it mean if anyone/everyone knew? Why does it matter?

Chapter 7

Making Sacrifices

"Love is unselfishly choosing for another's highest good."

— C. S. Lewis

Since we've been talking about making hard choices, why stop now? By now, you are challenging yourself to step out, stick with it, be authentic, love out loud, and expose your true self, unashamedly. Don't be surprised when you feel like you have to give something up to attain this *higher calling*. The calling to evolve. In this chapter, I will challenge you to sacrifice your comfort for *growth*.

FREEBIES

I love free stuff. Yesterday I discovered its "Free T-shirt with your purchase over $100" at my favorite nutrition store this month. I relish in telling my husband, "Look, honey; it was free!" By now he knows I'm teasing him. It's always met with a chuckle and, "Oh, baby, nothing is free." He had to help me see that there is always a cost to the free thrills I was showing off. It was discouraging, but I came to understand it as true. Now I say it for a laugh. At first, I wanted to appeal to his frugal nature with my "free hand massage" with my manicure. He wasn't impressed. Almost everything with any value has an upfront cost of your time, money, or effort in some way. I think we are all looking for freebies and shortcuts. Life is hard and costly. And no one has it all. If you know someone whom you believe has it *all*, let me assure you, they are sacrificing *somewhere*.

During my years as a stay-at-home-mom, I joined a gym because they would take my babies for two hours a day (free with a membership!). I didn't care if it was a gym, a Bible study, or a root canal—if you were going to take my kids off my hands, I'd stand on my head for two hours. I got into it pretty quickly, discovering that my strongest desires were toward beastly kinda stuff like heavy lifting, box jumps, and medicine ball throwing. The more muscle I gained, the more I ate. And ate. And ate. I was bulking, but I wasn't really seeing the same definition as some of the other ball busters in the gym. I researched and got to know physique competitors and took loads of advice and guidance from blogs and my most toned and defined gym-rat friends. I learned that diet was pretty much *everything*. I learn that until you melted the fat off the newly gained muscle mass, you would never be "shredded." This began the long war between wanting to be ripped and wanting to eat at pizza buffets. I was an all-or-nothing, on-and-off the wagon dieter. I would have bouts of strict eating (and by bouts, I mean approximately ten days), followed by the ever-faithful voice in my head saying, "Screw this."

After several years of trying to figure out which master I would serve—ripped body or enjoying sugary pleasures—I chose one. I ultimately decided I was not willing to make the sacrifices necessary to be shredded. I grew mad respect for my physique-competing friends. They are willing and able to sacrifice gluttonous behavior and even many social gatherings for that beautiful win. They have earned and deserve the applause and moment of glory for what I found to be too insanely difficult of an accomplishment. Oh, how I wanted to look like that. But the price was high. Too high for me. I admire the dedication and self-restraint it takes to achieve it. It's just not a sacrifice I'm willing or seem strong-minded enough to make. And if you found yourself working on your physique during the days of the "strong is the new skinny" mantra, like I did, I hope you realized how misleading that advert is. Did you ever notice the ripped woman on the poster board for this saying? She is strong. She is also what? That's right. Skinny. So go ahead and get strong. But it doesn't always look like her. Nor do you owe it to anyone to look like that.

For our purposes here, we will define sacrifice as *giving up something you love for something you love more*. Some common examples include:

1. Giving up money, certain foods, or social engagements for a winning physique.
2. Giving up your yacht for your child's college education.
3. Giving up your career to raise your kids.
4. Giving up your Saturday to serve at church.
5. Giving up your boyfriend for your self-respect.
6. Giving up your sleep to comfort your child/encourage a friend/ raise money for a charity.
7. Giving up your time to volunteer.
8. Giving up porn for your spouse's peace of mind.
9. Giving up alcohol for weight-loss/safety/being emotionally available.
10. Giving up the past for your present happiness.

Sacrifices promote the greater good of another or yourself. It's a tradeoff of something for something better. A sacrifice is not trading something less desirable for something desirable. That would be no sacrifice at all. It's typically something we don't necessarily want to part with.

YOU DID WHAT?

One of my more memorable mommy fails was giving one of my four-year-old daughter's stuffed animals to a little girl whose daddy had just been killed in a car accident. I don't regret my decision, but I wasn't considering my daughter's stage of development when I made that hasty move. Young children at that age are only beginning to think outside themselves and consider another's wellbeing. I didn't really have time to think about it in the moment, still reeling from the shock of learning about the death that required my presence as a senior Spouse. Talking about it with my daughter a year later, I'm pretty sure I lost some of her trust. I tried then, and still try today, to explain the meaning of her sacrifice and how her loss may have brought some comfort to this sweet child. She isn't having it. She's simply in a developmentally self-centered stage.

Maturity—we'll define maturity as the ability to delay immediate gratification in favor of long-term best interests. Impulsive behavior, or not thinking through a decision or its consequences, is a benchmark of immaturity. Maturity is a biological function and can't be rushed. It's a product of the brain still continuing to form, which, according to recent research, takes until age thirty now. Being immature is nothing to be ashamed of; it's just part of human brain development.

We just need to survive these impulsive, self-centered days that make up the first third of our lives. How do we do that? I truly believe there is no right or wrong answer. I used to think, *Maybe God wanted all people to get married and start working at age twelve and bypass this self-indulgent adolescence period altogether.* Then I thought, *Maybe adolescence is necessary for educational purposes and figuring out what you want to do with your life, but since we aren't supposed to have sex before marriage, everyone gets married at like twenty?* Then

I thought, *Ha! Thank God I didn't marry anyone I dated before age twenty-eight!* You think about this stuff when you have daughters. I mean, how are you going to advise them? The answer is not that simple. It's more about making sure they know God, follow God, obey God as best they can, and most importantly, *talk* to God.

My single Christian friend whom I'll call Hannah found herself in bed one morning with a man she hardly knew after a fun night on the town. He was beautiful, the chemistry was hot, and she struggled to regret any of it. Later that day, she worried that God was mad at her for enjoying herself in this manner. I asked her if she talked to God about it. "No. I can't involve God in my sinful behaviors."

"So you're just gonna pretend God didn't see you?"

"I doubt God was there or that God would want to hear about it."

"I'm thinking God was and would like to converse with you about this."

Have you ever said, "Oh, no, Lord, look what I've done"? or "I think I need you to rescue me right now," or "Oh, Lord, I'm sorry, but it felt so good." These are conversation starters. I'm not suggesting you go out and live haphazardly. I'm suggesting you don't leave your God out of it. I'm never going to be able to make my daughters walk the straight and narrow or get married at the age I think right for them or make them go to college if they want success in both marriage and career. What I can do is make sure they have opportunities to know God well. God is the way, the truth, and the life, no matter what road you choose, when you choose it, or how many times you fall on your ass going down it.

ANYTHING FOR LOVE (BUT I WON'T DO THAT)

True love requires sacrifice. People don't really want to hear that. They want the excitement, the butterflies. Many women want the *day* they are entitled to, when Prince Charming chooses them, the *one*—the groom gets lap dances paid for by his buddies the night before, the bride wears white, has a long-awaited bonding moment with Dad, the groom rocks a tux and makes Mom proud, the couple's loved ones lavish them with praise and presents. It's *their* turn to have the Cinderella story. They *deserve* it.

I teach a pre-marriage class once a month. I am always in awe that no one takes notes. They actually think they're going to skate through on this lovey-dovey feeling for the next fifty years. They have no clue what they are getting into. Most of their struggles will begin at the first moment of sacrifice: giving up time spent with buddies, "your" side of the bed, input on decorating the house, etc. The real display of love is *what you are willing to give up for the greater good of this sacred union or for the other person's excellence.* We do this in marriage, parenting, familial relationships, worship, and sometimes, friendships. Tithing is an act of worship or showing God love. Parting with money isn't easy for anyone, which makes it sacrificial. Ten percent of our income should come second to our love of God. Otherwise, you're just saying you love God. Pony-up and prove it.

WAIT. SHE GAVE UP DRUNKEN, ONE-NIGHT STANDS FOR THIS HOUSEWIFE BULLSHIT?

I chose to sacrifice all other lovers when I got married. And my husband has never made me regret it. I'm guessing most wedding vows still include "forsaking all others" as the lifelong promise you make to the one who is standing with you in front of God and everyone you know. But I don't remember feeling like I had an option. I anticipated marriage to the "one" most of my life. That's what you do. Anthropologists suggest it only took a couple of centuries for us, as a race, to transition from hunting and gathering as a tribe that needed to stick together to farming. We became property protectors who valued keeping our own seed in our own soil. This move away from nomadic life led to monogamy, which is a way of creating social order in an otherwise chaotic fight for rights to family treasures and land. Is it natural? Most people I ask vehemently say no. And I tend to agree. But I chose monogamy and still would today.

When I ask my husband why he is monogamous, he says, "That's a choice I've made." What I want to hear is, "There is no one better than you; you are the only one I can ever imagine being attracted to or wanting." But it is a choice. And actually, I'm kind of glad his devotion to me isn't based on an emotion or attraction that may wane. My husband and I choose monogamy because that value has been instilled in us. Like I said, I didn't even consider any other way. This was always part of my definition of love. Sacrificing the fleeting, flirty, butterfly feels of that first electrical connection to another possibility and to be seen in a new, fresh way by longing eyes is something I chose to forgo (take that, ego!) But just because you choose to be a vegetarian, doesn't mean bacon stops smelling good. I see this sacrifice as something *sacred*. If you're in a traditional marriage, you joined an institution where membership required an oath before God to love that person, no matter how you feel in any given moment, shooing away all others.

I think even polyamorous couples strive to keep the sacred in their relationships. These types of non-monogamous relationships are growing in popularity. My generation has a hard time separating polyamory from the douche-baggery of cheating. I don't personally understand how folks come to agree to these terms. But I am from a different time. I get the longings to branch out, but only in total secrecy, which I can see would appear unhealthy to the polyamorous. It is easy to end up longing for someone else. I have many close male friends and will honestly say they give me something that my husband cannot always give me: unconditional, positive regard, no matter what choices I make. How easily I could romanticize this disillusioned connection. But they have nothing invested in my choices. They have nothing to lose by supporting my lavish purchases or watching me drink too much.

CURIOSITY KILLED THE COUGAR

I understand the temptation to get caught up in a sexy tryst outside marriage. I met middle age by clutching my youth. Of course, this affinity for maintaining a youthful image is known as the ego, which is the perceived self or false self. I once had a single best friend who was dating around. We hit social hot spots quite a bit, and since I'm a good friend, I had to help her strike up conversations and have a good time. As it turns out, I still had what it took to attract a twenty-something. A year previously I would have doubted it because when I was visiting a new mom in the hospital with a onesie in hand, the maintenance guy in the elevator asked me if I was visiting my grandchild. As a result, my ego was satisfied with more nights out reclaiming my youth.

The more I indulged in my false sense of self, the less happy I became with the real, genuine love I had at home—enter *the mid-life crisis*. The sense of false-self or ego tries desperately never to die. This is why people will war in their relationships. Needing to be right is in defense of this false sense of self. The false self is particularly at risk of dying as we age. Any sort of identity crisis is fueled by a preoccupation with the past or future self. We seek experiences that support who we were or who we'd like to become. It's our mask. It's an imagined self and is disingenuous. It wreaks havoc on relationships, peace, and joy, and always leads to regret. It is also responsible for us tending to care too much about what others think of us. People will either support our ego or threaten it. We recover from threats with selfies, bragging, and pretending (and attracting twenty-somethings).

The ego is a powerful force. It needs to be recognized before it can be challenged by your True Self. What is your True Self? It is the un-masked part of you. It doesn't respond in anger, jealousy, judgment, fear, embarrassment, shame, and anxiety because it has nothing to lose or hide. It's not saving face. It just is. It's the *you* right now. No ex-pectations. It has no story because it's not based on a timeline, whereas the false self is the *story* of you, including all your accomplishments and failures.

A midlife crisis is a disruption to your story.

A midlife crisis threatens who you think you are or want to be. It is a period of holding on to how you perceive yourself. Acting as if you are still that person instead of crossing over to a new and improved self-story, one of wisdom, sensitivity, altruism, and being an awesome grandparent.

I got curious about what was happening inside of me that made me so uncomfortable with the next stage of life. Why was I longing for my younger self? Why was I so protective of the things of my youth? Why was I so triggered by signs of aging? I wanted to embrace this stage of life and be happy. But the younger me (the one I thought was the real me) was desirable, strong, free, and fun. I still had many of those attributes, but I felt them slipping away. Why? Because the ego doesn't want to die. It will go to great lengths to survive. My ego was the younger me. My true self was me *right then*. And why was that so bad? I had a loving family who embraced aging. Why was I clutching to this youthful identity? I am me right now. The ego was protecting the story about me, the sense of myself as being valuable when I am desirable, strong, thin, athletic, pretty, and so on. What did I risk losing if I gave up these attributes? My favored self, maybe.

With any luck, people will eventually embrace the transition and invest in their positive self-image by valuing things like wisdom, sensitivity, compassion, and altruism that grow with age, not societal expectations based on looks. And let's face it, when my friend asked me if I was flattered that a twenty-nine-year-old dude wanted in my pants, I said, "No. Just because I have the equipment to get him off doesn't make me special." I don't get my self-esteem there anymore. I really have grown. Don't be tempted to get your value in the most undeserving places. I just needed to get over my *old self*. How about you?

SUMMARY

Sacrificial love is typically what is required of us, as expressed throughout the Bible, to demonstrate our love for God. We are asked to trust God with our money by sacrificing at least 10 percent. God asked for plenty of animal sacrifices and even someone's child in the Old Testament. (Don't worry; God didn't let Abraham go through with it.) What are you willing to give up for someone you love? God's only begotten Son was given up for us—the ultimate sacrifice, freeing us from condemnation. Without sacrifice, love is just a feeling. Let me encourage you to stop saying you are sending thoughts and prayers someone's way and actually pray for that person and/or provide a service like a hot dish or a real hug.

EXERCISE

1. What is something you love that you want to sacrifice for something you love more? Can you do this with joy in your heart at the thought of knowing it is a genuine expression of Love?

    _____

    _____

    _____

    _____

2. What stories do you find yourself holding on to, perhaps retelling over and over?

    _____

    _____

    _____

    _____

3. Are you leaving God out of parts of your life, waiting until you get your act together before renewing your relationship with God?

    _____

    _____

    _____

    _____

4. Whom do you think you are (competent, capable, mature, intelligent, kind, selfless)? How does protecting this image cause mental or relational tension?

    _____

    _____

    _____

    _____

Chapter 8

Choosing Peace

"Your life becomes a masterpiece when
you learn to master peace."

— Unknown

YOU SUCK

A woman I'll call Peggy, who was new to Christianity, phoned me
for a counseling session. About four years earlier, she had discovered what the Lord had done for her, how Jesus loved her, and that
God had plans for her life. She eagerly came into the faith, repen-
tant of her ways, and was baptized in the Holy Spirit. It was a joyful
time full of relief and gratitude. And, of course, the celebrations
on earth were dim compared to what, I believe, was happening
in Heaven. The thought makes me ugly-cry at every baptism I attend—I don't even have to know the person. Before long, Peggy
eagerly began to dig deeply into Scripture, wanting the whole *truth*
and to know how to serve this amazing God. She listened intently
to sermons, joined Bible studies, learned how to pray, what to say,
and more importantly to her, how to be worthy of God's gifts.

As a self-proclaimed *doer*, she not only wanted to serve and honor the Lord, but to get it *right*. Her eagerness to please God was a humble reminder for me. The intensity and fire she felt to make herself deserving of such love, and to make sure she was honorable, was endearing and special. When she came to me for counsel, she was in much distress; she despaired about her inability to stay focused on prayer, having negative thoughts toward others, and remembering her awful past that she wasn't sure she could actually be truly saved from. As a doer, she worked more diligently than ever to pray, question, read, serve, honor, and obey. And then she hated herself when she felt incapable. What these negative thoughts were, I don't know. Old recordings from her past, Satan whispering accusations, or just a fleshy tendency to be lazy, preoccupied, negative, and unsure. It was probably a mixture of all these things, but they were certainly interfering with her ability to be a good Christian. She was growing weary and discouraged by her inability to offer anything positive—even friendly smiles were becoming tiresome for her. The light of the world! What?

Peggy was experiencing the phase of her Christian journey that I refer to as "discovering how bad you suck." I remember this agonizing part of the journey—the grieving of my sinful nature—the recognizing myself for who I truly was when trying to live up to God's standard of perfect holiness. I sucked, and I was fit to be tied because God was not transforming me more quickly. I tried super-hard to muster feelings of kindness toward others, energy to serve on top of going to church every week, courage to tell others about God, and seeing others without judgment. So, here I was, mad at God for not making me worthy, mad at my parents for not going to church every Sunday, and mad at myself for being me. Anger isn't exactly a motivating factor in becoming a light to others. I was down on myself.

Luckily, the journey doesn't end there, and God didn't leave me there. But that phase of the journey is a very necessary part of learning how deficient you are before experiencing the complete and total reckless love of God. After you accept that you suck, grieve your nature, and fall back into God's loving arms, you will be even more in love than you were at first sight. The difference will be that the works will flow more freely out of love, effortlessly, and you will never, ever give yourself the credit for it. All glory to God for the rest of your life.

Only God gives a degree of peace that we can't even fathom. "The peace of God, which surpasses all understanding" (Philippians 4:7). You can't explain it. Life is a shit-storm, yet you're at ease. Finding this peace is a byproduct of trusting and resting in Jesus and His ridiculous love for you. This does require a bit of a choice and forward movement—steps of faith. My action toward this was the simple daily prayer, "More of You, less of me." I longed for this. I felt bad about myself when I bit people's heads off, judged my friends, and swore in front of my children and other people's children. God always seemed to speak back to me, "Be still and know that I am God," or "My Grace is sufficient for you." What a loving response. You're off the hook; I'll love you no matter what. Be still my heart. Thank you, thank you, thank you. Praise God. My cup overflows with things I *know* were not in me, nor ever will be in me alone.

SURRENDER

Now, don't be too surprised when this cup overflows one day and is bone dry the next. Relationships require consistent attention and action, even with God. You have to communicate, have faith, ask, submit, surrender, and obey. Not because you will earn God's love, but because you love God and want God's will to be done. The love part has to come first or we are just gonna clang like cymbals (1

Corinthians 13:1) and get frustrated with ourselves again. Surrender is a loving gesture. It's a show of trust at a time when we are full of doubt, insecurity, anxiety, and really, really, really wanting our own way. This never comes easily, not even over a lifetime. It's a relationship of push and pull, talking out the nonsense, waiting in the madness, and trusting. The thing that often discourages me most about myself is that no matter how much God has worked out all things for my good and clearly had a plan, I find it almost as hard to trust the next time I have to "let go and let God." It never seems to get any easier.

Peace is not the absence of struggle. It's the presence of love. One of the more insane peace-robbers is expectation—of others, ourselves, and of God. We have an idea of how we want things, how we want folks to act, and what we should or shouldn't think or feel. This is hard to let go of, right? How do you accept unknown outcomes or simply "what is" without trying to control or manipulate? You must lay it down, in a sense. Trust the unknown to a known God. We need to be present and know that we are not in control of the past or future.

BEING PRESENT

Stress and anxiety, which I believe are the opposite of peace, are a result of the split between being here and wanting to be there. It may be the past or the future or a different place. But it isn't reality. Reality is happening now, and God is now. God is "I AM" (Exodus 3:14), meaning "here," right now. God is not in your anticipated, imagined future; God is here in the present. We worry about things that are not happening to us right now, forgetting that God is not there. It *is* a scary place. If we know God is here, we have the strength and resources to deal with troubles as they occur. Not before or after. We spend way too much time regretting the past or worshipping it—anticipating the future, or worrying about it. Remember the story I told my eight-year-old about sending her away to college? Mindfulness of your current surroundings is paramount in surrender. Otherwise, we are calculating and assessing and wondering, as if to gain a sense of control or preparation for things. Maybe healing in this area for you is to and not harm you but give you hope and a future (Jeremiah 29:11).

YOU DON'T NEED DOUBLE Ds TO BE HAPPY

The wandering mind is our autopilot mode of functioning, and it tends toward the negative. Left undisciplined, inebriated, unstructured, it subjects us to a constant barrage of negative thoughts all damn day and night. You set yourself for failure most when you *drink* during *downtime*, or as I call it "the Double Ds leading to doom." Choosing peace is a matter of staying present, surrendering control, trusting, and minimizing cost/reward (we'll discuss these in the next section). Fortunately, we are in charge of our brains, not vice versa. We can wake up and take the wheel. This means noticing our minds are adrift, and redirecting them to what we can control: what's right in front of us. The wall you're painting, the gun you're cleaning, the boot you're shining, the child's story you are listening to, the road you're driving on, and so on. We can carve out times to plan for our future and maybe even discuss some of our past in weekly therapy sessions, but the predominant state of mind should be in the here and now.

Your life is now; you are now; God is now.

During the day, shift your focus as often as possible to your surroundings, noticing the look and feel of what's around you—maybe the floor under your feet, the breeze in your hair, the sand in your toes. It's meditative and very enjoyable. If you're in bed, let go and sleep. If this is too hard, focus on your breathing. Feel your belly rise and fall as you take breaths. Stop the brain from moving along the time spectrum. God says, "Go to sleep. I'll stay up and worry about it." That is Love.

STRESS MUCH?

Sometimes we just need to say "Enough." Do you have trouble saying no? If so, learn to do it like your mental health is at stake. It is. Treat your mental health as precious and sacred space. I got good at realizing which of life's demands were optional and which were required, which would cost me and which would reward me. If the obligation costs you your peace, it's too expensive.

Here's an example:

When I got engaged, our courtship had been quick and intense. Why would I ever let the stress of planning our wedding day ruin the fun? I wanted high passion, low stress. The only thing that threatened to ruin my passion was a stressful wedding day that wasn't going as *planned*. For what? I was so in love; I didn't need everything to be perfect. I even told my fiancé, "The minute this gets stressful is the minute we decide to get married in our jeans in my backyard." Simple as that. I knew my limits and chose "no stress." Obligating myself to put on a show and entertain my family members was optional. The cost (stress) wasn't worth the reward: a perfect *display*. I just wanted to feel swept away and completely unaware of my surroundings. I chose accordingly. For me, it was the right choice. I had a great day.

Get good at stating what you will and won't be a part of. If a playdate this week will stress you more than relax you, don't go. If you're not up for an argument, choose to be happy over right and concede. You don't have to set yourself on fire to keep anyone warm. Learn when to rest. It's a commandment. God needs your tank full, not running on fumes.

I know not all stress can or should be avoided. But that's just reason enough to minimize it where you can. Delegate household chores, say no to some social events, forget the homemade casserole and bring a premade rotisserie chicken to the potluck. Pack light, keep a day planner or to-do list, turn The Weather Channel off, and keep the Facebook comment to yourself. Think about what you are allowing to drive you nuts. Do you panic or grit your teeth in traffic? Why? You're stuck. Choose not to stress.

It is what it is.

My daughters can be little drama queens. I frequently have to remind them that they are actually *not* starving; they are hungry. The situation is inconvenient, but not life-threatening. Are there things you possibly exaggerate, making them far harder to tolerate than if you put them in their proper perspective? Be careful not to buy into situations or circumstances as "horrible" or "impossible to cope with." You don't have to be a victim in your own mind.

ARE YOU HIGH?

My mom has been wheelchair-bound for twenty years. The deteriorating Multiple Sclerosis began its course long before then, but it has slowly and progressively gotten worse. What's so remarkable about this woman is her most pleasant demeanor, bright outlook, and consistent good mood. Many people over the years have stopped me to ask if I was sure I was hers. They also note how incredible her outlook is despite her circumstances. She has faced being excluded by her friends because of the difficulty she has getting around on her own. Her dependence falls fulltime on my dad, who has his own ailments, including deep and debilitating arthritis. Their sex life was disrupted, their income shrunk, their travel plans were annihilated, and plans of helping with their grandchildren mostly vanished. Their house had to be remodeled. Mom had to learn to use her left hand only. She was in and out of the hospital with complications, and she could no longer cook, clean, take a shower, or do her hair or makeup.

No way would I, in the same situation, be anywhere near as graceful as her. She's always smiling, never complains, and never, ever engages in self-pity. She's an enigma. I always assumed it was the medicinal marijuana, but I found out she never used the stuff. I was mystified watching my dad struggle to move her. But my dad was the only one who knew what to move, when, and where to keep her from falling. Every once in a while, she'd get a cramp or he'd misplace a foot, and she would scream out in pain. Sometimes, she fell, and then my dad would have to call my sister to help him pick Mom's dead weight up off the floor. My sister got trained to move Mom, but with me living in another state, I was never able to help out. I was only able to watch these situations play out from a distance. It is a horrible thing to see your parents struggle. I felt so bad for them.

One time when I was there, we finally got Mom up off the floor, and as her crew worked to get her back into her seat, she announced "Careful!" in anticipation of having something turned the wrong way, causing her to spasm or go rigid and immobile. When she had finally plopped back into her seat, she burst out in a small, sweet sigh, looked up at me smiling, and exclaimed, "Glad that's over!"

I was still holding my breath, searching her face for signs of hopelessness, trying to think of the right words to console her. Nothing. *Okay, that's it*, I thought. *What gives?*

"Mom? How do you bounce back from all this so quickly and without any traces of bitterness?" I asked her.

Her reply: "The Serenity Prayer."

"God grant me the serenity to accept the things I cannot change,

The courage to change the things I can,

And the wisdom to know the difference."

It's simple; it's easy. It is what it is. I can't change it, but I can control my attitude from here on out. The disease has taken a lot of freedom, but it has certainly not taken her peace. She has some say over that. A lot, if you ask her. I get it's hard. I'm a stewer. I'd be swimming in self-pity, resentment, jealousy, and rage. She has captured the present moment, let go of the past moment, and chosen to trust and accept she is not in control. Are any of us?

PEACE WITH YOUR PEOPLE

Is there any *one* who rocks your peace of mind? Leaves you seething for a day or two? Love doesn't keep a record of wrongs (1 Corinthians 13:5) because peace cannot exist in a build-up of betrayals, slights, jabs, and resentment. Rehashing those things in your brain is throwing fuel on the fire. Who's the worst enemy—the person who inflicted the pain, or you for continuing to replay it over and over? You're breaking your own heart at some point by keeping the insult or attack alive. We will talk more in Chapter 16 about forgiveness of bigger offenses, but for now, the stuff we can blow off, wherever possible, we should. Your sanity is at stake.

When I got married, I got all kinds of advice. "Never go to bed angry." "Eat dinner together at the table." I don't remember much else. But I do remember one that made a big difference: "The key to a happy marriage is short-term memory loss." Boy, was that accurate. It is simple, but not at all easy. I'm accustomed to stewing over injustice and insults. Add in that I'm definitely accustomed to winning and we have the perfect storm. I'd fester over comments for days. Some for months. When I thought about how hanging on to this stuff was affecting my mood, I started to understand that short-term memory loss advice. Some couples like to brown-bag these past affronts and use them as future weapons. This is what couples' counselors call dirty or unfair fighting. Like my mom, you have to get into the now by switching your focus to the moment instead of scrolling through your laundry list of past word vomit. We ruminate on things in part to maintain our self-image. It can be very infuriating to be thought of as wrong or misunderstood. And we will jump to our ego or false-self's defense at any cost. Even if we have to prolong the argument in just our own mind. *Who do they think they are? I deserve better than this. I can't handle this. What a dick face.* Fuel, meet fire. One can feel justified to indulge in these entitled thoughts and expectations, but the cost is high. Choose your battles; sometimes being at peace is better than being right. As a cognitive therapist, I urge clients to interchange phrases such as "He should have…" with "I would prefer if he had…" when judging a person's behavior.

SUMMARY

Choosing peace is often a matter of letting go and accepting what is. But you know this. It's only a concept for most. It is put into practice by paying attention to the current moment. Noticing your surroundings is engaging in your life. Present moment awareness is also about choosing life. It doesn't exist in the past or future; it is right now. Reach out and touch something. Notice your breathing.

Pay attention to what you are doing, even small tasks like walking up steps. Notice each one. Remember, tension is caused by being here and wanting to be somewhere else. Be present while you journey and while you wait. Make "It is what it is" a mantra. Try to notice times when you are anticipating the future or talking about the past and instead choose life. All you ever have to or can deal with is right now, in this moment. Don't let your mind just run on autopilot. Focus on what you are grateful for. Even if it's just the ozone. The negative mind tends toward what is missing or lacking.

EXERCISE

1. What will I let go of this week?

    _____

    _____

    _____

    _____

2. What five things am I grateful for?

    _____

    _____

    _____

    _____

3. What is one task I can forgo to get the rest I need to keep going joyfully?

    _____

    _____

    _____

    _____

Chapter 9

Having Fun and Being Joyful

"Never get so busy making a living that you forget to make a life."

— Unknown

Let's take a pause from all this growing and get down to the real reason you get out of bed every day. Have you ever thought about your *raison d'etre*, or *reason for being*? For me, it's to have fun, seek out adventure, and find something new. I'm not going to dig deep here; I know there are massively higher purposes for human existence that we can't even fathom, but I am driven to seek out fun and excitement, and it has made all the difference in my quality of life.

MATTER OF PERSPECTIVE

Perhaps because I was the youngest sibling, or because I had fifteen first cousins who all grew up around each other, or because fun was important to my dad, I have become accustomed to enthusiasm. I'm a bit of a draining battery always seeking a new charge. My husband sometimes refers to this as my "black hole" mode, never getting its fill. I'm kind of like a kid in a candy store. If I believed in past lives, I'd say this was my first time here. I want to try it all!

Having been happily stationed at Fort "Lost-in-the-Woods" and in Hawaii, let me assure you, having fun is a matter of perspective. But you have to look for the positive, be creative, and have an adventurous mindset. I'm talking good, old-fashioned fun, not gluttony, not hedonism. I don't think you need to indulge every fleshy desire until you get your fill. I never had to resort to illegal behavior to obtain my fun (although my second disorderly conduct was peeing in public, and my friends and I still laugh about it, but besides that). Just turn the music on loud, give me a beer, a hotdog, the sunshine, a pool, yard games, and good friends, and I am set. But circumstances rarely allow me to engage in that perfect scenario. A pool would help.

Since the perfect scenario can be hard to come by, we need to see fun as a state of mind, and I think I can help you find it or fake it, whatever the situation calls for. If it's not your default to find it or bring it, you must make a conscious decision to do it so that life doesn't become only a chore. Fun is your reward. It brings value to your existence. And people feel a gravitational pull toward this particular characteristic in others, so it makes sense that to succeed socially, it helps to be fun. And like anything else, it can be learned if it doesn't come naturally.

I had to teach my husband how to high-five. I mean, a good, old-fashioned "give it to me hard," put your whole body weight into it, grunt while you're doing it, high-five. Why is this important? Because it makes me like him more. Sharing in each other's enthusiasm is paramount to a good relationship. It's hard to define fun. You have your own definition of fun. But if you feel like there is a constant black cloud over you no matter what exciting thing is going on around you, you may be depressed. Ask your family doctor for a checklist to see if you have the symptoms and may need medicine to help lift that cloud. Some folks are just in a slump. Sort of going through life's tasks on autopilot. The people having fun are awake, engaged, energized, and smiling in the present, fun moment. People are drawn to fun people because they are intrigued and tempted to also wake up from their comas. What does this person have or know that I don't? Why are they so happy?

CAN YOU HAVE FUN?

Some people amuse themselves in isolation, some are the life of the party, others like to participate in social fun, and some people just don't recognize the word. When I asked my husband what he does for fun, he said, "I don't know." I said, "I'm doing research for my book; try harder." He put his book down, looked up at the ceiling for a moment, then back at me, and repeated, "I don't know." I let him off the hook. Two nights later, I was struggling to organize my thoughts for this chapter. I asked him again during our evening walk to the mailbox, "What do you do for fun?" He knew I must be getting exacerbated by now, so he searched himself a little deeper. "I don't know if I have 'fun.' I do many things that bring me satisfaction and joy. But I don't think I have fun."

"How did you manage to choose the most fun girl *ever* to marry if it wasn't important to you?" He jokingly said, "Because I knew I could change you."

My husband is funny, but he's right; he's not fun, at least in the way I define it. You may relate to this. Either you or your partner is fun and the other is not. I've seen marriages fail for lesser reasons. It can cause quite a rift. I used to call my husband "fun-buster." Now I only say it when I'm angry and don't mean it. I appreciate my husband more than ever. He is not a fun-seeker. He is thrifty, observant, rational, reasonable, tolerant, and methodical. He is a great counter-balance for me. I get the spotlight, all the entertainment funds in the budget, and he keeps me safe and the family thriving. I used to think he stifled my fun, but he has made it entirely possible. And where I turn more reserved around my daughters, my husband is chasing them around the house with a squirt gun pretending to be fun. Later, you and I will talk marriage and perspective—they go hand-in-hand in creating harmony. By perspective, I mean that if we can only view events and people differently, and see their outstanding qualities instead of focusing on what is missing, we can gain a new appreciation for them.

ACTUALLY, I CAN

I'd rather have a pap smear than play *Candy Land* with a three year old. Some grown-ups actually seem to be enjoying themselves when they play with kids. Like most observations, this leads to the thought, *WTF is wrong with me?* I'm like the most fun person I know. But I'm a fun *grownup*. Where's my inner child? Truth is, I don't think I have one. I hate roller coasters, water slides, and sand. And if I never see slime again, it will be too soon. This is why I had two children—so they'd have a playmate.

But if you have ever experienced parenting-guilt, you'll know I had trouble sleeping at night knowing damn well that *I'll miss this one day*. The same people who told you to "Enjoy your sleep now" while you or your partner were pregnant, inflict this "You'll be sorry one day" mentality. Thank you for the heads up; my quality of life is already improving with that warning. But no matter what I did, I couldn't enjoy myself. There was this tension. The same tension that we've already discussed in previous chapters: being here and wanting to be there. The first step in enjoying anything is to…

…be in the moment.

Kids are great at this. All sense of time is lost. The streetlights are on before they know it, and that means the fun is over for today, at least the running around in the neighborhood part. We need nudges to wake us up from wherever it is we are trying to get to. Playing becomes your current task, not a distraction from whatever tasks are calling out to you. If you even want to find fulfilment in playing with your kids, you must engage in it fully, getting out of your head and forgetting about what you *could* be or *should* be accomplishing.

FEAR OF MISSING OUT

What are you afraid of missing out on? Maybe the laundry awaits. Maybe you spot that handprint on the TV screen. Maybe social media is calling out to you. Maybe the thought of getting dirty or listening to the crying when you win or having to keep your child on track is simply not enough to make you be *still*. Remember sacrifice? Remember staying in the now? Remember trusting the process? You are building something miraculous, little by little, through every interaction with your child.

My oldest daughter's love language is so obviously quality time. She begs me to spend one-on-one time without "her" (referring to her sister). She wants to cuddle, read together, watch *Full House*, play UNO, window shop, anything—as long as she has me to herself. I know that lack of these experiences would be so detrimental to her feeling valued and connected. In the past, sometimes I struggled to be there for her. What was standing in my way? It was pretty simple really. My compulsory feelings of needing to *do* something, accomplish stupid tasks. Until I could get a grip on this, I wasn't going to enjoy a lot of "silly" or "mundane" things in life as well as miss chances to make memories.

What do you struggle to enjoy? Perhaps it's any social function or your job. Maybe it's waiting in line, walking your dog, working out, cooking, cleaning, or getting your hair cut. Ask yourself: Am I here or somewhere else? How can I accept and even enjoy this moment? What do I need to pay attention to and surrender to in this moment instead of force the outcome? The adventure in whatever you are doing is there, inside you, waiting to be embraced. It's not in the circumstance or situation; it's how you *decide* it is. My coworker and I one day realized we would look back on this time and be like, "Man, that job was the shit." What a wonderful thing to recognize! It was an actual moment of awareness that we had that was so good, despite being at work and not having amazing days every day. We took note of the little pleasures—our peaceful surroundings, our sharpness of mind, our amazing teamwork, and "the few and the proud" we get to work with.

Some of my favorite memories were made while stationed at the worst possible locations—spots that people refer to as "the armpit of America." Why? Because people came together to create fun, play games, host potlucks, build campfires, and tell stories. My husband and I took pleasure in perusing Walmart after church, and making late night dessert runs to Cracker Barrel. Nothing thrilling—just simple pleasures only made possible with the right attitude. "This sucks" would have been the beginning of a hellacious two-year assignment for us both. Challenge yourself to get a few laughs in between you and your hygienist next time you get your teeth cleaned. Change your perspective and look for the opportunity to grow or brighten someone's day. Perspective is almost *entirely* responsible for your quality of life.

There are many times when keeping this perspective can be difficult. I once had a client return from vacation with his wife and her family. He was very much looking forward to it when he left, so I was surprised when he returned, sat on my couch, and said, "Vacation sucked." My mind immediately identified two potential causes for his emotional state. Either everyone was inflicted with a stomach bug the entire time, or he was resistant/fighting the course of the vacation rather than accepting/embracing it. Fortunately, I guess, it was the latter. He explained the difficulty caused by everyone wanting their own way, getting sick of each other, and debating plans. It sounded awful. He didn't get to do most of what he wanted, and multiple fights with his wife ensued. I wondered to myself if he had just embraced the moments rather than resisted them, would it have been as awful? Could he have accepted what was happening and at least had a decent time? Vacationing with others is hard, and will ultimately fail if met with constant resistance because there are likely going to be conflicting ideas about what it should look like.

I woke up in the same house on Christmas morning for the first thirty-nine years of my life. How remarkable! Even as an Army spouse, we managed to cross the miles to get back home for my family's traditions. It has now been five years since I've been home for Christmas. The first year could have very well been the toughest since it was a profound loss and threatened my identity. Living in England at the time, we spent Christmas in Spain. How miserable, right? Well, it could have been. I was in a foreign country, far from the East Coast, and it was hot and sunny. It sure didn't feel like Christmas. I knew my perspective was going to make or break my experience. No one would blame me for being partially happy and a little homesick. After all, I was supposed to be with my family in Pennsylvania, freezing my ass off, and drinking beer with my uncles. Happiness is 50 percent what you experience and 50 percent your attitude about what you experience. I could accept and embrace what was or resist and fight it. I decided I was going to be happy—100 percent happy.

KNOW YOURSELF

Has anyone ever asked you, "What do you do for fun?" Did you really know? I created a quick inventory to find out what you do for fun. I was really determined to get an answer from my husband. Turns out, it's managing our money. To each their own.

Think of an activity that you do. It may be daily or once a year or somewhere in between. Ask yourself these two questions:

1. Do I do it with relative ease? (It may take some thought, but fun should just seem to come naturally and be free-flowing.)

2. Does it energize me? Give me a charge? (Fun should give you a second wind.)

This is what you do for fun. Let's take a look at a sample inventory and see what passes the test for you. I've answered the first couple.

Activity	Energizing?	Easy?
Running	No	No
Board games (with adults)	Yes	Yes
Driving		
Playing a particular sport		
Drinking		
Socializing		
Couponing		
Sales and marketing		
Reading		
Amusement parks		
Competing		
Painting (walls, pottery, canvases)		
Dancing/singing		

Cooking
Cleaning
Binge-watching a good show
Entertaining
Writing/journaling
Playing the stock market

CELEBRATE

The second step in having fun is celebrating yourself or someone else. Celebrations make people feel important, loved, and valued. To celebrate someone has got to be one of the highest gifts and compliments you can give them. My college roommate Stacie is the master of celebrating. Having worked at the Hallmark Store in college, she knew there was a day for everything from "Best Friends Day" to "Sweetest Day." She would delight me and the other roommates with greeting cards for things we never knew to celebrate. But in her world, there was always a reason to celebrate, and she knew just how to do it. I've always envied the way she dotes on people, including myself, when they have a baby, win a bingo game, or cut their hair short. She is the most celebratory and up-lifting person I know.

No one wants to be around a negative person, but misery loves company, and sometimes we get stuck. If you're reading this book, chances are you'd like more joy and laughter in your world. I'm doing my best to make you smile, but I know life and thoughts will soon take over. Can I encourage you to celebrate something this weekend? How about the life of your beloved pet that just passed away? Do you know someone with a birthday coming up? How about making it extra special for them by surprising them with balloons? People don't expect this kind of treatment as grownups, and it means the world to some, no, most people. Maybe your friend got a new job. Maybe you lost two pounds. Maybe it rained during a drought, or it's the first day of summer, or the last day of winter, or…you get the point.

THE GIFT OF ENTHUSIASM

Sharing in fun together energizes relationships. Bring an enthusiastic attitude. Enthusiasm is a gift you give to others. Take an inventory with someone close to you to see what things you both agree are fun. My husband and I have the most fun together at wineries. We love to taste the different varieties and compare thoughts. We also love a good show. While stationed in Fort Leonard Wood, we traveled to Branson to see Legends in concert, and we watched the entire series of *Lost.* You know you're energized when you stay up until three in the morning for just one more episode and meet back at the house during lunch to squeeze in another. The enthusiasm came easy. We were both super-stoked to engage in these activities.

But do you bring enthusiasm when you don't feel like it? If the range of enthusiasm is Debbie-Downer to Tigger, the majority of us are somewhere in the middle, and we often move up and down along the scale depending on what the situation provokes in us or calls for. We can either easily get excited or we *turn it on* for those involved. It comes naturally at times and is a well-timed social skill at others. When I meet a general's wife, a new boss, or a spouse who looks uncomfortable at an event, I turn it on. When the four-year-old neighbor girl tells me she rode her bike without training wheels, I turn it on. I put on my biggest smile and become a little more effusive than is my default. This puts people at ease and helps them feel good about themselves. It's a social skill, and an important one if you care to make an impression, make friends, or care for others. It's a *gift* when we neither feel like being enthusiastic, nor feel the need to gain approval. We simply want others to feel enjoyed. Let me explain.

I began to think about this attribute about ten years ago when my friend Sally took a call during a playdate with our toddlers. The conversation sounded like this:

"Hi! How *are* you? (smiling) That's awesome! Good for you! (laughing) Oh, my gosh, that is funny! Thanks for calling. Have a great afternoon, see ya later, sweetie. Bye." (still smiling)

I wondered whom she was so tickled to hear from. "Who was that? Your mom? Your grandma?" "No, that was Ted" (her husband). He wasn't deployed, mind you; he was at work and expected home in a couple of hours. I was speechless. I couldn't imagine ever speaking to my husband in that cheery tone. What was wrong with me? Why wouldn't I? When my sister calls, I increase the joy in my tone. When my best friend calls, I express great happiness to have heard from her and delight in her successes, big and small. My husband usually gets, at best, a half smile, at worst, attitude. Why was I reserving my enthusiasm for anyone who wasn't my spouse? It's as if my coworkers or the moms on the playground or the bank teller were worth more to me. Isn't this the way, though? Well, it's not really fair. We need to shine on those closest to us too!

The second time my laziness in this area occurred to me was when I was having sex with my husband. For whatever reason, I wasn't getting into it. I was tired or not in the mood and maybe distracted. I laid there thinking about how I would bring my A game to the gym all week. It would involve near physical torture that I would endure and embrace for a solid hour to attain the goal of a tighter, leaner body. I would push myself to the brink of my capability all for my own joy and empowerment. My fellow gym-rats would get my motivation, high-fives, and enthusiasm. Why was my husband getting the barely-there leftovers? Sex is so incredibly important for the health of the relationship bond, and I was being stingy and lazy. Withholding affection and/or enthusiasm is unloving and sometimes a form of passive-aggressive punishment. Let's have fun, celebrate, and show some enthusiasm in our lives. You will leave the world a brighter place.

SUMMARY

As a senior Spouse married to a Military commander, I was responsible for organizing multiple social functions. My motto has always been: If it's not fun, why do it? Truth is, many people feel inhibited when attending gatherings of many kinds, particularly those with a political feel. I like to bring the fun and make events worthwhile to all, even for those who are uncomfortable with most gatherings. We need people in our lives to learn and grow. Many people won't come together as a group without the promise of fun. This may involve eating, ice-breaker games, door prizes, alcohol, a bouncy house, whatever. But challenge yourself to bring the fun, or at least a smiling face and willing attitude. We could all use a few more happy gatherings, don't you think?

As a bonus, here is a sample list of the most fun songs ever. Crank it up:

"This Is How We Do It"—Montel Jordan

"Party in the USA"—Miley Cyrus

"Dancing Queen"—ABBA

"Footloose"—Kenny Logins

"Push It"—Salt-N-Pepa

"You Shook Me All Night Long"—AC/DC

Now go have fun and lose your shit tomorrow. Then read Chapter 10 to help you through it.

EXERCISE

1. What do you do for fun?

   _____

   _____

   _____

   _____

2. What do you have to celebrate in the near future?

   _____

   _____

   _____

   _____

3. In what activities could you lovingly show more enthusiasm?

   _____

   _____

   _____

   _____

Chapter 10

Managing Anger

"Wars begin in the minds of men, and in those minds, love and compassion would have built the defenses of peace."

— U Thant

While you're out trying to have fun, assholes will cross your path. That brings me to rule number one about managing anger: Don't call people assholes. Labeling others as *bad* in any way only deepens your contempt, and then everything they do will infuriate you. Truth is, there are some cruel and self-serving people among us. But sometimes we are too quick to label when we really need to spend more time with that person to understand them. Sometimes you need to excuse behaviors as growing pains. God asks us to be at peace with others, "if at all possible" (Romans 12:18). But even God knows it's a challenge.

"Haters gonna hate."

— Proverbs 9:8 (my paraphrase)

Let's take a look at anger, this difficult emotion, and how to thoughtfully manage your reaction to it before you flip your lid and screw everything up.

ANGER IS YOUR FRIEND

Imagine a life where nothing made you angry. Like a hypnotized Peter in *Office Space*, you go happily about your life, unaffected by the provocations of your dastardly coworkers, neighbors, or society in general. You could peruse social media with a blasé attitude, shrug off the fight-pickers, and stroll calmly through political debates. Sound glorious? Yeah, I think so too.

The degree of your ire depends largely on past situations that are imprinted in your memory as #don't-let-that-shit-happen-again. Anger is one of those "Wake up!" alarms that alerts you to situations that *feel* eerily familiar to prior bad situations. It protects you and others. Situations where we feel we have been taken advantage of or in which we see someone being treated unfairly will trigger uncomfortable feelings ranging anywhere from perturbed to enraged. It is a well-meaning alarm system spurring us to take action, defend our boundaries, or speak up against injustice. The *you* who comes out in response comes from your internal protector (amygdala). Sometimes your amygdala needs a talkin' to from your sensible self (prefrontal cortex) that knows there either isn't a real threat or knows how to use its inside voice when your protector is about to blow. (Hint—the amygdala is the first-responder because its intention is to keep us safe. There's no time to dick around. It takes at least twenty seconds for the sensible self to notice what's happening and respond with more socially-acceptable, not to mention legal, actions.)

Traumatic experiences are burned the deepest into our memory bank. They are situations that were actually or were perceived as life-threatening, whether the life of the ego or the life of the physical body. These experiences include combat situations, being cheated on, lied to, hit, car accidents, being bullied, and so on. The experience led to profound vulnerability of the ego (or sense of self) or the physical body. The protector urges you to fight or flee. When we experience reminders of these events in our relationships, we tend either to react in a passive way (flee) or an aggressive way (fight). Either reaction robs you of your sense of being in charge of yourself. And in a way, you have lost power to the first responder. It has taken over to take care of you. Unfortunately, what happens is we shrink back from opening our hearts to other humans for fear of feeling panicked, being rejected, self-loathing, and nightmares, and we sink deeper into what we may label as depression and anxiety.

LEFT OF THE BANG

The good news is, although you will never forget what happened, or be able to erase it or go back in time and explain to yourself that you will be okay, you can begin to notice your first-responder triggers, deal with the feelings in the moment, acknowledge what is overtaking you, and begin to soothe yourself and come back from the response. Only then can you start to speak clearly on your own or another's behalf and stand a chance at promoting change and being taken seriously. Otherwise, you risk reactions you may later regret. When we react, we retaliate, scream profanities in front of the children, put others down, put our fists through windows, get drunk or high, or spread malice. Maybe we go into hiding. Military folks call this preventative work "staying left of the bang," meaning to avoid an explosive, messy, regrettable reaction. It's doesn't mean to swallow or ignore, but to get in front of the brewing issue by acknowledging it and dealing with it.

Anger responses are sometimes ignited by feeling supremely vulnerable to a past offense. Either the physical you or the story of you (ego) is threatened, leading to hostile responses. Everything in our bodies resists this perceived destruction. Even if the perpetrator or threatening event is long gone, the feelings are what we've become afraid of. Having been bullied at a young age, I became physically reactive to mean girls. In high school, I would gain feelings of power back by fighting them. This is how I got my first disorderly conduct charge, in case you were wondering. I overcompensated for feeling weak by exuding a false strength. I learned to acknowledge the vulnerability within, change irrational thoughts, and speak assertively on my behalf rather than fume and fantasize about revenge.

NOW WOULD BE A GOOD TIME TO BE ANYONE BUT ME

As an Army Spouse, I've been obligated to engage in multiple partnerships with other men and women to support "family readiness." Some of these relationships came easily; others have been more challenging. For everyone, some relationships click, some spark. The most complicated relationships are the ones in which the other person triggers you. The response may feel like your heart is pounding in your throat; you may feel shame or rage. Once this happens, it gets very difficult to speak truth quietly and confidently. We typically want to fight or flee. Have too many of these people in your life and you'll risk checking out or engaging in unhealthy, numbing behaviors. I'm great at coaching folks through these awkward or tumultuous encounters—when my own emotions aren't involved. But I'm as reactive as the next person when I get triggered.

In my defense, I don't tell people to fuck off like I used to, but my default now is to disengage, and it's not helpful when I'm faced with a relationship I'm expected to be in with another. Expected relationships can be with another Military Spouse, coworker, small group participant, in-law, etc. While I believe you should avoid toxic people as far as humanly possible, sometimes you need to stay in the ring and be brave enough to work through the experience.

I would have loved to have had what it takes to deal with anyone without being triggered. Perhaps I would gently confront assholes in private, show compassion for what they were possibly feeling inside, and de-escalate every situation perfectly. I know these skills. I *have* these skills. But when we are triggered, the brain turns animalistic. Mine too. A coach can help you respond appropriately, and perhaps de-escalate the situation because their own emotions aren't fogging things up.

I hope you can avoid people who trigger you. I hope there aren't many of them. I hope when faced with the ones you *have* to engage with for the greater good, you rise to the challenge. I don't want you left triggered and checked out, or resorting to unhealthy, numbing behaviors to cope with all the anxiety. I could have used a counselor who wasn't emotionally involved to coach me through rough encounters. I know exactly what it looks like—*for other people.* I know I can help you navigate similar relationships when your heart is in your throat and I'm not the one being triggered. Then I'm a great asshole-whisperer.

OUCH. DON'T TOUCH ME THERE.

Notice what happens when someone threatens your status or trust, reputation or value. Chances are you get a little (or a lot) hot under the collar. Maybe your heart starts to beat faster; maybe your jaw clenches. The next step when you feel like this is to *surrender.* Accept what is happening and *pause.* Take a few minutes to talk to someone about what is happening if possible, or if not, write it down. Take deep breaths to calm your well-intended bodily reactions down and let the information work its way to the prefrontal cortex. If you've been drinking, this may take hours once you've stopped drinking. Ask yourself why you are so mad. What is your anger defending—an image of you that is in question to others? (Are you caring too much what others think?) Why are you defending this image? Maybe it's defending the rightness of your stance. Why the strong need to be right or have others concur with you?

Anger always comes second to a primary, more vulnerable feeling. If I want you to think I'm a rock star and my husband says something that embarrasses me at a social function, I will boil on the inside. Anger is urging me to strike back, say something to promote my bad-ass-ness again. I will likely do this by embarrassing him back. Why? Because I have a self-image. I want to impress. But when someone gets a laugh at my expense in a social setting, I'm embarrassed and feel unvalued. Satan is so ready for me to lose my shit and even whispers in my ear, "You don't have to take that. Do something."

But when I take a minute to notice my anger and ask myself what's happening at a deeper level, I may acknowledge rejection, unworthiness, and shame. Where another wife may blow off her husband's jabs in public, I am infuriated. Why? Because I have triggers that tell me I'm not good enough for him. My ego wants to believe I'm better than anyone he could have chosen. Now we have a problem. I have to know my triggers, or I will lose my shit every time. It's quite embarrassing having heated arguments with your spouse in front of your friends. And it's not necessary if I can express to him at a later time or in private what those comments do to me (the primary, vulnerable feeling) and ask him not to do it again. In the meantime, I continue to do my work on this trigger and heal the original wound that was created long before my spouse came into the picture. Maybe I need to ask myself why I have a need to impress or intimidate. It is most definitely a function of the ego, or *false-sense of self*—the story I have made up about myself to feel good about who I am. I'm a confident woman who deserves to be heard and respected. And as long as I believe that, the devil on my shoulder will make sure my pride is big enough to defend that story at every turn and squash anyone who doesn't support it. But what if I were already worthy, accepted, righteous, and approved of in the eyes of my Lord. Would it really matter then what you think of me?

YOU'RE MAKING YOURSELF MAD

Have you ever said, "That makes me so mad," or "She pisses me off"? Well, technically, that's a thinking error. The activating event or person may say or do something that triggers a self-thought, but it's the thought that makes a person angry. Otherwise, the same things would make every human angry. But why is it that when your friend's spouse says something that you think should infuriate them, they casually blow it off? Why do political people anger some but not others? Why do other parents seem to tolerate whining more than others? The answer is because they are telling themselves something completely different about the situation than others. Some things that would frustrate them might not bother you for a second. Once we grasp this idea, we can have more patience with the activating event or person, and then with the people around us who don't share in our fury, because let's face it, we get baffled and even more frustrated when others don't see things the way we do. Either they are strange or we are. Either they are unacceptable or we are.

What are some of the thoughts or beliefs that make us mad? Here are a few:

- You *always* interrupt me when I talk.
- You *never* like to cuddle.
- You're just a jerk face!
- You think you're better than everyone!
- You can't do that!

- You are wrong!
- This is horrible!
- Men suck!

Here we see a lot of extreme thinking, labeling, mind-reading, rule-setting, absolutist thinking, catastrophizing, and over-generalizing. It is our belief about the person or event that makes us angry and determines our degree of anger. Instead of combatting and controlling the person or event that *seemed* to make us furious, we can figure out the recordings in our brain that, in fact, determined our emotion.

You are your own problem and *solution.*

Once you've been triggered, tell yourself what you believe about what happened and write it down. See any irrational thoughts or exaggerations? Irrational anger is one that causes us to fight for our ego. Legitimate anger causes us to speak up for injustice or set a healthy boundary. Let's take a look at the actions that caused a woman to carve a sentence into my car last month.

THANK YOU FOR NOT SWEARING

I was in Costco-hell, looking for a parking spot so I could get milk, eggs, and chicken at a discount, and perhaps win a bit of hubby's approval for that day by saving a buck. I spotted a truck in a parking spot with two gentlemen unloading their cart into the bed. Since there was no one behind me, and they seemed to be moving at a speedy pace, I decided to sit and wait for the spot. They pulled out; I pulled in. I get out of my car, and begin to make my way to the front doors when a woman in a monster truck I hadn't noticed previously yells out her window to me, "Hey! Didn't you see me waiting for that spot?"

"No, I didn't. Didn't you see me?"

"I think you did see me."

"No, I sure didn't. Sorry," and I carried on toward the doorway. I didn't hear what she screamed next, but something about a key and car. Whatever, I was determined to go inside without an episode and put it out of my mind. Me-1, Ego-0.

The next day, my children alerted me to the writing on my car that I hadn't previously noticed because it was on the passenger side. It said:

"I didn't see you, sorry."

"This was no key job," my friend, Raul offered. "This was a nail, screw, or knife job." It was deep. And I knew where it came from. So, let's take a look at what this woman's anger led her to do, all in the name of vindication of her ego. In the beginning, she was a little more than annoyed by losing the spot she thought was hers. She was irate. I can only assume her belief was somewhere along the lines of not being treated fairly. She decided to confront me, which is still in the realm of acceptable, since maybe I would be more courteous or aware next time. Maybe my apology would have been enough to feel like the universe was balanced again, but no such luck. Her irrational beliefs caused her to plot revenge. Let's theorize what she may have been telling herself:

- "Fuckin' Haole." (non-native)
- "She did that on purpose."
- "She probably thinks she got the last laugh."
- "I'll show her."

Truth is, I didn't see her, and I thought it silly to get back in my car and move it for her at that point. I was actually kind of sorry, but I just freaking hate Costco and was trying not to lose my cool. I couldn't wait to get home, and she was kind of scary in her big-ass truck. But her beliefs set her over the edge. She *hated* me and was going to show me. Damage done. Thank God she didn't dig a curse word into my car because I wouldn't have been allowed on base until I got it fixed.

CALL ME JUDGE JUDY

Do you ever assume what people are thinking or doing and make your mind up about them on the spot? Of course you do! We all do. We are constantly judging situations, trying to decide what's good or bad. This is why we got booted from the garden. God didn't want us to go around thinking we knew good from bad, right from wrong. The human heart is deceptive, y'all. We rely on our own interpretation of things and are usually way off. Only God knows the heart of a person, what led them to any given point, and where He has yet to take them. Vengeance is not ours.

Trust in the Lord with all your heart and lean not on your own understanding; in all your ways submit to him, and he will make your paths straight.

Proverbs 3:5-6

Imagine you're teaching a class or giving a presentation to a crowd and you notice someone in the audience yawn and put their head in their hands. You assess the situation and conclude what? Are you an awful and boring presenter, or did they not get enough sleep last night? Who knows? But what you *tell* yourself about this behavior will determine your feelings and response. Perhaps you will call them out in front of everyone and embarrass them. Perhaps you will assume they are sleepy and ignore it. Perhaps you will assume they think you are boring but that it doesn't make you a *boring person,* so no biggie.

Other ways we make ourselves angry is by determining how things *should* go or what people should do. It's a bit of a God-complex when we think we know how the world should work. You would be better to think in terms of the way you would *prefer* things to be, without deciding the way they *ought* to be. This belief leads to an indignation that leaves little room for others to have an opinion. It separates people rather than brings them together. It is the endeavor of the ego to create enemies and divide people. The ego enjoys creating and having enemies because it loves being *right*, not at peace. Some Facebook friends make enemies anywhere they can. They love to rant about everyone from the hairdresser to the security guard to their siblings. There is *you* and then *everyone else*. The ego gets stronger by opposing others and complaining about others, and ultimately, over enough time, it detests many people. Do you ever operate on this level? Think about a time you complained about a waitress or store clerk rather than accepting the situation. Why do you think you chose to feel irritated and *right* over accepting and being at *peace*? Did your response improve or deduct from your quality of life?

PASSIVE OR AGGRESSIVE?

I believe confrontation is difficult for everyone. That is why making bold statements from behind your phone screen on social media is so appealing. I get to speak my mind without having to look you in the eye, show my nervousness, or risk getting a throat punch. Confrontational situations put you in a very vulnerable place. You risk looking like a fool, being rejected, proven wrong, losing your cool, crying, throwing up, passing out, and getting arrested, hurt, or laughed at. It is the job of the amygdala to fight or flee. Therefore, the natural reaction in approaching situations where you need to call someone out, set a boundary, ask for what you deserve, or work out an issue is to shrink away from these or similar situations (passive) or come on super strong and demanding (aggressive). Your tendency is to be at either extreme, and it is a learned social skill to be *assertive*. People who have not learned this skill and are not getting their way at either extreme will creatively engage in a combination of the two, called passive-aggression.

Before we talk about the preferred skill of assertiveness, let's take a look at the nature of passive-aggressive (PA) behavior. The most basic way to explain it is to describe it as the tactic of one who is not honest with others about their anger but will dole out punishment in disguise. The PA person doesn't directly or privately confront anyone, but leads others in their tirade against someone and comes out feeling like they somehow won. Have you ever seen these passive-aggressive Facebook posts pop up on your newsfeed?:

- "Some people don't know when to stop."
- "Does anyone else think selfies are ridiculous?"
- "Well, I've read enough right-wing bullshit for one day. Signing off!"
- "Someday, you won't have a mom/sister/daughter and you'll be sorry. Jus' sayin'...."

There are so many other ways to be PA that it would take another book to explain in any great detail. Where aggression is getting your way by using power, intimidation, insults, and boundary invasion, passivity is wimping out altogether. To be PA is to get even, or send a message in a way that disrespects another and can later be denied or blamed on someone else. It can range anywhere from harmless sarcasm to spreading wicked rumors and is completely ego-serving. Normal people sometimes pretend they're unaffected by others when they are really seething beneath the surface, but PA people will plot to get even and you may not know it. If you suspect them, they can easily deny it by claiming ignorance. It's an underhanded way to express hurt by getting back at the person who hurt your ego without appearing irrational. Children who are discouraged from or even not allowed to express anger will often resort to this means of expression. This fact helped me tolerate many more fits of rage from my children. I was a lot more accepting and helpful because I knew that shutting it down altogether could cause some very icky behaviors.

A few examples of normal, less slimy PA behavior include unloading the dishwasher sloppily, making vague social media comments, "forgetting" to do something, showing up late, withholding affection, short answers ("Whatever," "Fine"), and claiming "I was only joking." I think all of us can relate to some degree.

I FEEL YOU ARE MAKING ME CRAZY

Assertiveness is defying all of the above natural and comfortable ways of dealing with situations that require your voice. Because of this, I consider assertiveness the hardest social skill to learn: it's unnatural and takes great courage. It is often a reaction-formation that doesn't match the inside. We are either scared and dying to flee, or angry and dying to stab someone in the eye. I've listened to friends and clients rehearsing with people close to them, writing and rewriting, and trying desperately to get an assertive response just right before going into the conversation. Sometimes we have the luxury of time and listening ears to help us speak up in a way in which we are clear, yet respectful of the other's rights and boundaries. A close, listening ear can often hear our tendency to be PA. The receiver's rights include: personal space, the option of walking away, an opportunity to respond, sticking to the topic, having clarity about your feelings and expectations, requests rather than demands, and preservation of the receiver's dignity, reputation, and privacy. You may or may not get your way or a resolution in the end—you accepted that possibility from the outset. Your goal is to influence, not control.

A typical lesson in assertiveness training is using "I" statements. This requires you to own your reaction to another person instead of blaming them for being what you dislike. For instance, let's say your coworker annoys the crap out of you. They are flighty, talk too much, whatever—the possibilities are endless. This person makes you cringe either because they are annoying or rude. You have been swallowing your judgments a long time, and one day you blurt out, "You are driving me crazy. Do you hear yourself?" The situation went from passive to aggressive, one extreme to the next. You swallowed, then word-vomited both attempts to deal with the uncomfortable feelings and make them stop. But now you've got new problems. You are seen by the office as out-of-control—you put someone else down and increased the tension in the space for everyone.

Set boundaries by owning your reaction to others. Maybe some people push one of your buttons. It's *your* button. You own it, and you are responsible for it. Other people are not responsible for knowing your triggers. You can explain them in assertive feedback, but you should never attack others for pushing your buttons. It's *your* issue. Express your feeling and reaction and what you need to happen next. Perhaps, "I'm really overwhelmed by this conversation. Let's take a break." Make eye contact, but watch your body language. Make this statement calmly and firmly, never in a pleading voice.

MANAGE OR CURE?

Anger management skills are useful and do not take long to learn. When people come to me for anger management, we talk about combating irrational beliefs, breathing, meditation, avoiding numbing behaviors, assertiveness skills, and so on. These skills are the determining factor in many folks keeping themselves alive and out of trouble. Teaching these skills was often my role as a counselor to young military personnel. But what if I told you there was a *cure*?

A cure for anger? Yep. It's not one that short-term, solution-focused therapists spend time teaching. In most cases, we have only a few sessions to help you cope before sending you on your way. For folks with the time and endurance, we will consider the power of *compassion*. Remember that every angry reaction is a response to a feeling you are too vulnerable to express in that situation (i.e., embarrassment, fear of rejection, inferiority, unworthiness, unlovable-ness, and humiliation). Compassion is the ability to *see beneath the surface*. If you work hard enough, for long enough, you can erase your chronic anger by trying to see what is really going on with someone when they piss you off. Now, because we are not God, we cannot see the heart of a person. I don't even know if some people are evil and others are just hurting. But I know that the only cure for being angry is to have compassion. This does not mean tolerating people's bad behavior or engaging in it or even hanging around people who trigger you. It simply means letting others off the hook. For them? No. For yourself. When others are on your hook, they are renting room in your own head. Trying to convince yourself you are better than them or calling them cowards or other names and writing them off are normally temporary fixes. The thoughts will eventually creep back in; reminders will provoke you; seeing that person will put you on edge.

Let's say, for example, that you found out someone said something about you behind your back. Let's also say it's a good friend and you found out they told a mutual friend you can be an irritable prick sometimes. Ask yourself:

1. Can I be? Maybe that's fair.
2. Have *I* ever said something about a friend to another friend in the name of needing to vent?
3. Does this friend have a habit of routinely offending/betraying me?
4. Did I say something to hurt them?

This below-the-surface questioning will divert you from the road to prolonged anger. Being judged or name-called by a friend is not alone a deal-breaker. If you write people off every time they fail you or hurt you, you will likely end up very alone and stunted. If you are able to soften your heart and forgive imperfections, chronic anger will be a thing of your past. Let's test your understanding of this concept:

1. Your nine-year-old was at a sleepover last night and came home in the afternoon grumpy because they didn't get enough sleep. You try to keep things peaceful, but your child is not listening, smart-mouths you at one point, whines, and heck, throws a shoe at the wall. This is completely unusual and intolerable. You are about to flip your lid and send the little stinker to their room until next week when you remember the curative power of compassion. How can you regard his situation, approach your child, and manage this event?

   _____
   _____
   _____
   _____

2. A server brings your food out cold. Was it their fault? What might have happened?

   _____
   _____

_____

_____

3. A store clerk was rude to you. Do you know anything about
    them?

    _____

    _____

    _____

    _____

4. Someone cut you off in traffic. Were they out to get you, or
    could something else be going on?

    _____

    _____

    _____

    _____

You can manage anger by deep breathing, counting to ten, bringing
your awareness back to the *now*, etc., but the only cure is compassion. What judgments and triggers do you have and why? Have you
ever acted in a similar way to the person who is upsetting you? You
have faults and have made mistakes too. Maybe you've even done
something similar to what you are judging in someone else (we tend
to have a thin skin when our own failings are reflected back at us), or
maybe you are judging something that is completely different from
your faults. Have you ever said, "Well, at least I've never done *that!*"
or have you ever found yourself mortified to find out when someone
did something that you know damn well you've done before? People
generally aren't out to ruin your day—they may just have things going on you could never know about or understand.

"Let the one who has never sinned throw the first stone!"

— John 8:7

SUMMARY

There's not much you can do to keep anger from rearing its head, but you can acknowledge you are angry and think rationally about the deeper feelings you are covering for, express them if necessary/appropriate, and then let whatever it was go. Some folks claim that the media aims to separate, confuse, and scare the population as a whole. There may be some truth to this, though I don't follow it closely. But I can see how it could be very angering to believe that generalization. Heavy media followers who listen or read intently on a daily basis to support their case that they are right and another is wrong are great examples of how you can infuriate yourself. Many believe the media keeps the population focused on a catastrophic world in the hands of incapable people and debating and ultimately destroying relationships. The underlying feeling is fear; it's what the media does sometimes play upon, and the outcome is discord. I imagine evil sitting back and smiling while the daily good deeds and good works go unnoticed.

Both faith and fear demand you believe in something you cannot see.

You choose.

Anger that sticks around longer than it takes to alert you is damaging to you physically and to the world as a whole. Think about an alarm clock. Its purpose is to wake you up. You can hit snooze, but it will keep going off. You can let it beep and may even fall back to sleep as your body adjusts to the sound. The alarm clock has become useless energy that you have grown accustomed to. It's lost its purpose to notify you of a boundary crossing. It becomes something other than useful—it becomes antagonizing. It had one job: to wake you up. After that, it morphs into something else:

- Bitterness
- Resentment
- Hostility
- Hatred
- Violence

These are all punishments we continue to inflict on ourselves long after any given event ends. It's like taking poison and expecting another person to die. You either need to problem-solve and deal directly by asserting yourself and/or your boundaries or stop thinking about it and get back to the *now*.

What negative experience do you keep alive inside yourself on a daily basis?

_____

_____

_____

_____

"God, please teach me to speak the right words at the right time with the right tone so I can live in peace."

— My hourly prayer

Chapter 11

Winning People Over and Making Friends

"Ah, kindness. What a simple way to tell another struggling
soul that there is love to be found in the world."

— A. A. Malee

Let's face it; life is easier when people like you. You win people's trust
and confidence, and people gravitate to you. Many serial killers and
con-artists are known for their likeability and charm. They are, in
fact, masters at the art of manipulation. They don't actually have any
regard for the person they are wooing and, on the contrary, set out
to ultimately destroy them. I want to be clear that I do not believe
in or support this kind of fake seduction. But I do believe in stra-
tegically creating connections with others. I've been trained in this
regard, going into some of the most closed-system family homes to
do therapy where chaos and disturbance is at its peak, threatening a
child's physical and emotional stability. There is even a name for this
skill in Structural Family Therapy training called *joining*. This skill
is your ability to see people as they *want* to be seen, and ultimately,
forming an alliance with them to create change. But I've been an intruder in many other situations too, whether it be living in a foreign

land or attending a CrossFit class (some of the most welcoming and nonjudgmental folks, by the way). Some people put you at ease immediately—others, not so much.

It helps if you just immediately take the stance of *being* kind to others and shining *your* light, rather than showing up and looking for light and kindness. As opposed to scheming, self-serving manipulators, we want to draw people in for good. Manipulators draw people in and then figuratively slap them in the face. Don't do that. This chapter will show you how to entice the most suspicious and guarded people so you can lower people's defenses, positively affect their belief in humanity, create connection, and defeat loneliness.

THE ART OF MAKING (AND KEEPING) FRIENDS

I've moved nine times in fifteen years of marriage. I'm pretty good at making friends, but I've had to learn the following:

1. People aren't so much assholes as they are guarded and unsure. Many people are *looking* for a friendly face, not trying to *be* one. You be one. And you don't have to like everyone, but you do need to be courteous and polite, and maybe even kind and approachable. You might be surprised how this approach opens doors to friendships you never would have predicted.

2. Making friends is like dating. And it is equally exhausting. Every move we made meant periods of being on my own, a stranger to everyone. Within six months, I'd have set up multiple playdates and maybe even a coffee or movie with a few. By the end of the year, one or two of them had clicked. Within the next six months, I'd meet potential friends who were on their way out. By the end of year two, I would be on my way out. Believe it or not, I have made a lifelong friend at every duty station.

3. You will make more friends in two months by *being* a good friend than you will in two years by *looking* for one. Looking for friends sets you up for disappointment. As you weigh your options and scrutinize people's actions and non-actions, you will certainly find flaws and excuses to go back into hiding. Truth is, people can be dicks sometimes—even you. But looking for someone you like and wishing and hoping they might like you back is setting a standard that will ultimately lead to being discouraged with all things social. Also, remember that quality is better than quantity. Popularity was for high school. Spend your time and energy on your precious few, rather than spreading yourself thin among many.

4. If you build it, they will come. Instead of looking for friends, look for your *places*. *Where* do you belong? What environment? Maybe it's a Bible study, maybe it's work, maybe it's volunteering in childcare. These are your interests, and you show up to grow up. It's about developing yourself as a human. Maybe it's an environment that you want to learn about or challenge yourself in. A CrossFit gym, a college class, or a community class like oil painting or sailing. It's where you are curious about yourself and dig deeper to find out what you are really made of. After several weeks, you are certain to have started forming bonds with those alongside you whom you would have *never* gone looking for. My friend list ranges from all ethnicities, weights, ranks, genders, and ages. My closest friend in graduate school (pearls before swine guy) was a sixty-five-year-old, Irish dude. He sat beside me in class, loved pubs, and was a bit fatherly. Had I been scanning a room looking for my next bestie, I surely wouldn't have chosen him. But if you live your life okay with being alone, *find* yourself, and stay focused

on your mission, the most unusual folks will become some of your closest confidantes.

5. There are no rules. There truly are friends for a reason, season, and lifetime. You captivate people by smiling, making eye contact, and truly being excited to see them and get to know them. When you treat people this way, you'll have well-meaning acquaintances everywhere. You will have people who recognize you and even begin to seek you out solely for your demeanor and energy. Some of these folks may ask you to join them in another setting, perhaps getting to know each other a bit more. Things are generally light and good-natured. You are focused on making that person feel good about themselves and feel good in your presence. You are a blessing to each other, or maybe you are just a blessing to them (in which case, this person shouldn't be your only friend, but it happens). Sometimes people just need you more than you need them and vice versa, and that's okay; the world doesn't need to be all even-steven. Not all of your friendships will be reciprocal. Some folks will benefit from you more than you benefit from them and vice versa. We are all at different stages of life. I like to seek out people who know more than I do about stuff. But I also enjoy spending time with people I feel I can be a blessing to. No one person was meant to meet all of your needs.

6. You've developed a friendship when you've allowed flaws to exist, yours or theirs, and neither of you run for the hills. Tolerance for each other's flaws, idiosyncrasies, and choices is what friend-timacy is all about. You may go to this level with one or two, but it's where the *work* begins. If your tolerance for others is low, this is typically where you might decide you are "done

with the drama" and move on. But often, it's just that your broken pieces and their broken pieces may begin scraping one another. Healthy people know their own triggers and can also tolerate most people because they separate the person from the behavior. Unhealthy people often resort to a mentality of, "I don't like you, and I don't know why—it's you, not me—I don't need this drama."

7. If you are in a committed, romantic partnership, intimate friendships may need more boundaries. You are already working on intimacy in your primary or romantic relationship, so the time and energy spent on a close friendship can become draining. We express tolerance for our friend's actions by remembering that they are not our primary relationship. Their choices and way of being do not and should not affect our life to the degree that our primary relationship would. Bottom line, if you are not their lover, it's not your problem. Support, encourage, pray, give advice when asked, but you need never strive to make your friend anyone other than who they are. This will save you from internal strife and unnecessarily hurting the other person and damaging the relationship. Accept people exactly how they are. You are not the judge and jury in their lives. Save that energy for your romantic partner *if* they are willing to adapt and change for the good of your relationship and your future together.

Joining

Whether you're trying to make friends, make an impression, or influence someone, people will always be more receptive if they feel seen and heard. The first task is to identify how a person wants to be recognized.

Steven was the stepfather in a household I was working with. The patient was an adolescent girl with severe emotional disturbance. The stepfather/stepdaughter relationship was strained, and Mom found herself in the middle, struggling to influence her daughter positively, but not appear like a doormat to her husband who thought she took too much of her daughter's crap. She treaded very lightly, while daughter and husband only got angrier and angrier. Our therapy teams were authorized for eight months to join with and stabilize the family. Sometimes secrets were unveiled, exposing the family dysfunction and causing the patient to express symptoms. Other times, it was a simple but problematic dynamic that not everyone was adjusting to.

It was easy in this situation to identify who had the power. It's typically the person you would least suspect, but in this situation, it was clearly the stepdad. He was in charge, even though he would frequently suggest that Mom ran the house. We knew if we wanted to help this family change, we would have to align with him. If we, the outsiders, indicated in any way that he was responsible for the problem or the solution, we'd be the enemy, and the family would remain impenetrable. Before long, we were able to say:

"Stepdad's attempts to positively affect this family were often dismissed, and he was made out to be the villain, when all he ever wanted to be was a hero in these girls' lives."

Once we noted this aloud to the stepfather, we were aligned and the course was set for how we would help him with his original goal, despite the ingratitude he constantly felt. We *saw* him for who he was (or maybe, rather, *wanted* to be), and when he felt understood and respected, he became less guarded and teamed with us to change how he behaved in his role, affecting the way the family functioned. Lo and behold, multiple dynamics shifted, boundaries were set, the parenting alliance was solidified, and the symptoms of emotional disturbance decreased enough to keep the child in the home. The work is easy once you have the welcoming embrace of the person in power.

No one cares what you know until they know how much you care.

The skill of joining has come in very handy, not only in therapy situations, but various social and familial situations. Have you ever had an in-law seem to dislike you for no apparent reason? I joined an outrigger paddling club in Hawaii after living there for two years. Outrigger canoes have six-person crews, and racing them is the oldest sport in the state with deep roots in Hawaiian culture. Native Hawaiians tend to make paddling a family affair. Racing outrigger canoes is a beloved tradition that takes a lot of commitment and dedication. Technique is tricky to learn and typically mastered only after years of dedicated practice. Hawaiians regard the ocean as sacred, cleansing, and healing. There is a ton of pride associated with enduring the rigorous training, and ultimately, competing in the forty-seven-mile journey across the Kaiwi Channel from Molokai to Oahu.

I arrived at my first practice feeling like an overly eager "white girl," similar to how I felt at my first gym class in England. I was bright-eyed and dripping with enthusiasm. As in Britain, my countenance was sometimes met with awkward smiles or even suspicious glares. American and/or white women are often recognized by other countries as exuding confidence, being outgoing, and, well, enthusiastic when seen in the best light—and loud and obnoxious in the worst. I felt like I was in pretty good shape, maybe even someone to be considered an asset to the crew. I found my welcome anything but gracious. Maybe one person made eye contact. At practice two, one person introduced themselves to me, and at practice three, my efforts were noted with a nod. What was going on here? Did they not like me? Why were they so stand-offish?

Perhaps you too have been perceived as an outsider or intruder at some point. No one dislikes you without reason, even if they seem to; there is always something potentially threatening or assumed about you. You have a couple of possible responses here. I don't need to explain them; they will come naturally. The one you should choose is compassion. What's happening beneath the surface? Perhaps they are displacing a past experience onto you. Perhaps they are intimidated, shy, unsure, or know something about you becoming a part of the group that you don't (e.g., someone may lose a seat on the crew because of you). Once you look beneath the surface and consider the possibilities, you can approach people from a place of humility and perhaps make it a point to recognize the others in a way that puts them at ease.

I opted to keep my head down and work hard. I followed the cues of the others closely so I wouldn't be a burden. I showed an eagerness to learn what they were already so good at. And when I was told I couldn't race because of a hurricane canceling a qualifying race, my response didn't match my internal one. Although I was disappointed and felt I had made many sacrifices, I explained that it was an honor just to be a part of the team and learn the sport. And that was true. These women are rock stars. It took weeks to build my endurance to where it was even close to theirs. And they let me take a seat each practice starting day one. I was grateful to them, humbled by their strength, and made sure not to have an entitled air about myself. By the middle of the season, I was receiving high-fives for my efforts. And as you now know, that is my primary (up top) love language.

Had I approached the team or presented myself without humility and gratitude for the gift of learning this beloved custom, it would have been disrespectful and I would have lost the opportunity to continue learning, be up close to dolphins, see once-in-a-lifetime sunsets and rainbows, and be part of something so much bigger than myself.

INFLUENCE OTHERS; DON'T CONTROL THEM

If Facebook has taught us anything, it's that bashing, shaming, and guilting other people for their opinions will never, ever change those opinions. Another time we get caught up in autopilot is when we judge, disagree, and then spew. Ever notice how everyone admits their ideas or beliefs are horrifying and thanks you for showing them the error of their ways? Yeah, me neither. But just because we can't control people doesn't mean we shouldn't strive to *influence* them.

I was born wanting to change people. It's only natural that I became a therapist. This judgmental spirit and the expectations of being able to change people made me bail on some relationships too soon. Professionally, it led to quick burnout. What I have learned for my own mental health is that you are only obliged to ask someone with whom your life is bound to agree to change. This is typically your romantic partner and underage children. No one else is fair game. You're not "theirs," and they are not "yours." This is probably why I get couples in counseling and have yet to see my friends or acquaintances walk through my door. Although I wouldn't be opposed to it, and friends sometimes could use support in untangling from each other or communicating better, I suspect the sessions would be a bit shorter and a little more geared toward "you do you" and "you do you" instead of bending toward one another and compromising on deep-seated beliefs and habits for the sake of the health and unity of the relationship.

After realizing *who* I wasn't allowed to control, I realized that those who were fair game didn't really want to be controlled. What could I change then? The answer was my own expectations and accepting what is. I embraced the virtue of influencing others instead of trying to change them. You always have the ability to influence folks, but once you've decided how and when the change should come, if at all, you're back to being controlling and sitting on a throne that is not yours to sit on.

You must adapt what you expect from others. For instance, someone takes days to reply to your texts. You tell them this is annoying. They continue to do it. You get angrier and angrier, still expecting them to do something different rather than altering your expectation that they reply more promptly. If this person is your child, intimate partner, or employee, you may protest, establish boundaries, or set consequences. If not, you need to alter your expectations and plan accordingly. You don't have to "defriend" them, give them the cold shoulder, or keep losing your shit. You know that you actually have to call this person rather than text or simply rely on someone else when necessary.

SERVING VS. HELPING

Two roles influencers take that controllers do not is *servant* and *lighthouse*. Any time you find yourself in a helping position, whether it be bringing food to the elderly, giving financial advice to a sibling, giving parenting advice to a struggling friend, feeding the homeless, counseling a teen, making a meal for the sick, or cleaning your daughter-in-law's house, you are either in a one-up or a one-down position. How you conduct yourself when offering assistance puts you in a potential power situation. It is easy to see that there is a giver and a receiver—someone is wiser, better-off, more informed. This automatically undermines a human's right to dignity. People, including yourself, get stuck. Particularly those with struggles we are unaware of.

Working with the military, I hear a lot of, "Thank you for your service." I'm fortunate to have this reminder that the biggest and baddest people in this country are servants of its people, protecting their lives so they can enjoy the freedom to say and do what they feel is right. No life is greater or lesser than yours, no matter who has more strength and resiliency at the moment. We are here to *serve* others, which automatically puts them in a position above us. Helping means reaching *down* to another. Serving means they are above you, in an honorable position deserving of your service, especially your support when they have a moment of weakness. Never exploit the fragility of life by suggesting you are giving the *help* they are so "desperately in need of."

> *"So Jesus called [the disciples] together and said, "You know that the rulers in this world lord it over their people, and officials flaunt their authority over those under them. But among you it will be different.*
> *Whoever wants to be a leader among you must be your servant, and whoever wants to be first among you must be the slave of everyone else. For even the Son of Man came not to be served but to serve others and to give his life as a ransom for many."*

> — *Mark 10:42-45*

When my husband was selected for Command, my dear friend, a more seasoned Colonel's wife, hugged me, and said, "Congratulations, and watch your back." I gave her a confused look, but it didn't take long to realize what she meant. "People try and take down leaders. You'll see." And she was right. Sometimes, no matter how good your intentions, there are people everywhere with rebellious hearts. I'd like you to consider submitting, serving, and praying for leadership rather than spreading hostility, confusion, and causing division.

BE A LIGHTHOUSE

What do all lighthouses have in common? They stand still in one place, shining their lights for ships to make their way toward. They don't go running about the world seeking ships to save. That is not to say you shouldn't leave your comfort zone and travel to aid others, but it does mean being less frantic about who needs your assistance and not running the risk of infringing on people's right to autonomy. This kind of help generally comes from people-pleasers who are seeking ways to get their own needs met. These folks sometimes go home assured they did their good deed for the day and made a good impression in the eyes of others. The motive is wrong, and it may even be forced or fake.

Take into consideration those nearest to you who don't appear to need any light. If your mind is elsewhere, thinking, *Whom can I affect or touch today with all this awesome light?*, you may never realize that your coworker could use a flicker. Or maybe you could shine on the person walking toward you in the grocery store. Be aware of your surroundings, and slow your racing mind by getting in touch with your inner glow. Then shine *right where you are*. Don't grimace when you disapprove of how someone is ignoring their screaming child in the store. Flash a smile, for Pete's sake, and say, "Been there," or "I'm sorry. It'll get better; I promise."

SUMMARY

What makes controlling others so tempting? Duh! The *ego*, of course. Remember, the ego seeks to be right, divide, and make enemies. I'm always surprised by how many fans and supporters on Facebook the people have who rant and bash others. People actually encourage such behavior with likes and virtual high-fives, while making meaningless comments supporting the haters. Just remember, Adolf Hitler had millions of followers. Make it your leadership mission to walk into a room and bring light, putting others at ease.

EXERCISE

1. Whom do you provide help to whom you can count as someone you serve? How does serving them change the way you view that person? How does it change the way you interact with them?

   _____

   _____

   _____

   _____

2. Whom do you need to accept just as they are without trying to alter them in some way?

   _____

   _____

   _____

   _____

Chapter 12

Being a Team Player

"Good teams become great ones when the members trust each other enough to surrender the me for the we."

— Phil Jackson

A shit-ton of gasoline is not a problem without a match, nor is a match without a shit-ton of gasoline. But they make an explosive team—dangerous, illuminating, powerful, and impressive when paired up. The two elements of salt, when separated, are potentially life-threatening. Teamed up, they are life-enhancing; in fact, our bodies even depend on salt. Not to mention salt is a lovely addition to an otherwise bland situation. There is a greater good for all elements that cannot be achieved in isolation. Creating new life, loving, learning, growing, conquering, building, trusting, and, put simply, evolving require the presence of others in your life. In this chapter, we'll take a look at the life-enhancing process of working toward a common goal.

GOALS

I'm going to spare you any lectures on why being active is healthy and how sports build confidence and communication skills in children. You can google that stuff. You, as an adult or aspiring adult, are a team player daily, unless you live alone on a secluded island. Your role: to sacrifice personal glory for a common goal. Teamwork makes the dream work!

What is the common goal? Sometimes, it's meeting a quota at work or establishing a bedtime routine for the kids or even raising them. Maybe it's winning a relay race or some other competition. Maybe it's simply to love, give glory to, praise, or ask for something from God. The mission is to attain something of greater good, something larger than our singular, feeble existence could accomplish. Even Tom Hanks' character in *Cast Away* created a teammate that couldn't actually physically help him. He projected all that he needed emotionally from a teammate onto Wilson (a volleyball) so he could meet his higher goal of getting back to his love and life. Wilson challenged his decisions, remained committed to the task, and provided a common belief in the mission. Hanks' character and Wilson joined forces, and the eventual success was a team effort, make no mistake.

Sometimes the goal is to eliminate another team. There is something so innately gratifying about forming an alliance and "destroying" the opposition. (Then shaking hands afterward and congratulating them on their efforts.) The New Zealand All Blacks, a rugby team, do just that. Competition on the squad for starting spots at certain positions is fierce. Coaches make strategic decisions for the good of the team that may disappointment a particular player. For the All Blacks, Jersey 11 is the most coveted and sacred—made famous by super-player, Jonah Lomu. Recently, the head coach called on a twenty-year-old rookie to take that role over a much more experienced player. There was no room for ego. No time to argue who was better or worse or more deserving. You die to self, take your place, wherever that may be, and do it better than anyone, even if it's cheering from the bench. The mission is the greater good. The aim is the win.

This same dynamic often plays out between siblings. Parents are constantly contending with children blaming, tattling, whining about the other, and demanding fairness. But when siblings ban together against the parents, bonding and lifetime memories are formed. Sibling alliances are normal and should be respected, although not given authority. When forces align for a potential win, it creates an adrenaline rush. Actually, winning is euphoric.

EMBRACE FOR IMPACT

Mental toughness is when you can find fuel in an empty tank. The people who struggle alongside you during the most difficult periods of your life won't easily be forgotten, particularly if the battle was hard won. You may have experienced this during a deployment (yours or your spouse's), a sport, at the gym, or at work. Being a team requires people of all different backgrounds to come together, dress alike, or "as one" in some cases, and do something no one person could do alone. A group of people are set apart from others to accomplish the impossible. They have a unique purpose and belong to the mission in a way the "average" person doesn't. And I'm not talking about just our uniformed heroes; I'm talking also about the church choir, the high school basketball team, co-parenting or step-parenting, a softball team, and a staff. We are all working toward some greater good, even if it's just "winning" and giving the crowd a good time. Spectator sports create alliances like nothing else in our country. We want the win! Look at the crowd from the perspective of the blimp and you'll see a sea of the team's colors, all lining up in solidarity to support their team, the world's finest.

I was fortunate to be a part of a winning softball teams from age eight to eighteen. Those ten years were some of the best of my life, and every once in a while, I and some of my Facebook friends, who participated in those championships together, reminisce about the good old days.

We left dirty, sometimes defeated, but almost always proud and tro-phy-totin'. Running around second base while hearing my dad franti-cally tell me to round third toward home, or hit the deck, followed by enthusiastic high-fives and a huge, proud smile for knocking the ball so hard, are images I will cherish forever. Neither my husband nor I (nor anyone else for that matter) will ever be the softball coach my dad was, as much as I'd like to replicate that for my daughters. But I have incorporated that feeling into our family by making my girls put their hands together with mine and shout "Goooooooo, Emenheisers!" be-fore missions we participate in such as cleaning the house or going on a hike. They get the sense that we were made for excellence and are called to give our all for the team. Sometimes our family teamwork involves what I call "divide and conquer." We all must go our separate ways sometimes for the good of our family, God, and country.

GREAT EXPECTATIONS

There have probably been times when people have expected more or less of you. Teams typically hold us to a higher standard, which we might never hold ourselves to. If I'm at the gym, I'm not doing abs unless I take a class where someone makes me do abs. It's just a fact. I know I will work harder and do more with a coach than I would ever do on my own. I will push myself when there are expectations. My teacher knows that the words, "We're all in this together!" are a powerful motivating force. There's something special about not letting others down, sharing in the agony, and performing your best because people need you to. It is a privilege to be a part of accomplishing a mission, even when it means getting your ass chewed. You humbly accept all forms of motivation to help you support the team—the calling is *that* great.

I will also push myself harder when others' expectations for me are small. The ego likes to prove people wrong, and accomplishing a feat of some kind is a decent way to feed that need. No one loses their dignity; they just might be impressed or pleasantly surprised, and my ego will be doing cartwheels. She needs a little love from time to time, too. Do you know you deserve a crowd that expects you to achieve and demands more from you than you believe you have in you? I've said before that I seek out people who are better than me. They aren't hard to find. There are many people who are stronger and even more who are smarter. They will either push me to grow or inadvertently persuade me to push myself. As much as I struggle with all things critical in nature, particularly from my husband, truth is, he has standards that have encouraged me to be a better adult, a person I can be proud of. Shh…don't tell him I said that.

SUMMARY

Teamwork is an expression of love, if not *the* expression of love. It requires sacrifice and faith, which is love unfolding. This is why we often refer to our teammates as our family. We become one. God is a Team: the Father, the Son, and the Holy Spirit—Three as One. At the time I joined the outrigger canoe team, I found myself going home daily, drinking, and texting an ex-lover. When someone I never met before stepped into my life and offered a position with the crew, I could hear God whisper right in that moment, "You were made for more." And I knew God was talking about how I was spending my free time. Not surprisingly, I soon found myself on a team with four intensive practices a week, getting my ass-chewed and pushing myself. God is so cool.

We don't challenge ourselves by staying in our comfort zones. This becomes a question of, "Do you want to grow, or do you want to be happy?" Teamwork makes us bend toward others, build trust in others, prove ourselves trustworthy, lay down selfish desires, promote another and/or the outcome rather than ourselves, communicate clearly, give and receive empowerment to be our best, and deny ego. Sound fun? It's frustrating at times, agonizing at others. It's one way we deny the flesh and rise above our nature. The reward is great. Which is why I'll push a little harder in the next chapter.

If you want to go fast, go alone.
If you want to go far, go together.

— African Proverb

EXERCISE

1. Can you think of a time when you were part of a team and everyone celebrated a victory in the end? What was that like?

    _____

    _____

    _____

    _____

2. Where or who are your current teammates? What is the greater good you are working toward?

    _____

    _____

    _____

    _____

3. What is currently frustrating you in the process of "making the dream work?" How might you reach out to your team to encourage your mission's success?

    _____

    _____

    _____

    _____

4. Is there anywhere you can be a champion? Are there any teams
    in your community you can join where teamwork and hard work
    are more immediately rewarded—softball, rowing, bowling, darts,
    trivia competitions?

    _____

    _____

    _____

    _____

Chapter 13

Taking Risks

"Courage is the commitment to begin
without any guarantee of success."

— Johann Wolfgang von Goethe

I'm not a highly motivated person, but I am highly motivated to seek out highly motivated people. Being a good leader isn't always necessary. Sometimes if you want to get places, you should just be a good follower.

CAN YOU TAKE ME HIGHER?

I'm a member of a hiking group in Hawaii. Why? Simply put, because I would never go hiking otherwise. My husband and I are ambitious-enough people, but neither of us would be leading the other out the door on a weekend morning to go explore the beautiful hidden trails of Hawaii. We'd both be sitting our happy asses in front of the TV watching anything other than waterfalls. Visiting waterfalls is a nice idea and many, many people come here to hike the hundreds of unique trails with views you don't find anywhere in the world. Still, we're cozy on our couch in the air conditioning.

However, I don't want to miss opportunities, and that often means doing things I don't feel like doing. I don't want to get out of shape, but I also don't particularly want to eat healthy foods and exercise. This is why I sign up for gym classes. There are people who take on leadership roles in this arena, and I need them to tell me what to do. I used to be a certified personal trainer, so I know what the hell to do. But I *need* them to tell me what to do. I'm a great follower; I am front and center of the class, replicating every move the instructor makes. But I'm never going to go into a gym and lead myself into completing 100 squats. When I go to church, I'm front and center singing along with the worship team because I wouldn't do it otherwise. I'd rather play *Candy Crush* than read the Bible, so I join Bible studies to stay educated and drawn to God. It's normal to lack motivation. So find people who have the calling for something and do what they do. Let them inspire and catapult you into doing something you wouldn't otherwise do. Lead where your passion is to lead; follow where it's not.

THE COOLEST RISK I EVER TOOK

Remember Sheldon, my junior high bully? Last summer he reached out to me via Facebook Messenger when he saw that I was in his city visiting a friend. He lived there with his family and wanted to get together to "buy my family lunch." I was poolside by myself when he dinged my phone. My friends and children were in the pool. We had been Facebook friends for a few years by then. I wasn't holding any serious grudges since he often *liked* my pictures, and I figured he was somehow paying restitution for his childhood behaviors. He was married now, had a little girl, and had seemingly grown into a decent family man. But you can be certain he was a major player in my life. Although I wasn't bitter, my husband and closest friends knew of him. He was partially responsible for a lot of the insecurities I had throughout my teenage years and into my twenties.

When Sheldon so kindly proposed to buy the family lunch, I thought the offer was sweet, but I graciously declined. Most people are just being polite anyway, right? He didn't actually want to look me in the eye and sit awkwardly among strangers, right? Did he even remember how he had treated me? Did he think we were friends or something? I put my phone down and relaxed back into the sunshine. That's when my thirteen-year-old self started begging me to reconsider. Do you really want to let this opportunity slip way? Where's your sense of adventure? Where's your curiosity? Are you really okay with a superficial social media resolution with this person who so greatly affected your worldview? I would fly back to Hawaii the next day and *never know*.

I sat up and messaged him back asking when and where? I told him it would be me and my friends and children and that we'd be there in twenty minutes. I rounded up the troops, put my hair in a ponytail, and off we went. During the drive, I coached my conversation-dominating friend to keep quiet because I needed to hear what this man had to say to me. They agreed to keep the children occupied on the sideline while we had our moment, if there would even *be* a moment.

I was nervous walking in, but genuinely ready for whatever was about to come my way. Except that I wasn't. I walked in secure in who I was and who I had become and didn't believe his opinions of me, no matter what. He was waiting for me to arrive before being seated. We made eye contact, and I enthusiastically smiled and said hello as if seeing a dear old friend. We walked toward each other and embraced. It was unexpected, but not unheard of. He led me to a table after meeting the rest of the crew and pulled out my chair. He sat close by, looked me in the eye, and began to weep. I stood up to give him a hug and he reciprocated. I was smiling and even half-laughing because I was so tickled and grateful for his demeanor. "Karen," he said, "I am so sorry for how I treated you. I am not that person anymore." I held his face in my hands and told him I forgave him, hugged him some more, and drank peanut-butter beer and talked for the next hour. He told me about his childhood and his wife and daughter. He told me how he had been thinking of his apology to me for years. He had a friend in Hawaii whom he had thought about sending to my house with a gift and letter. He wanted it to be personal and meaningful. When he saw I was in Phoenix, he thought that was the perfect chance.

I don't know exactly what happened inside me that day. My adult self had already forgiven him and become secure and sure of herself. I believe I did it for that little girl inside. And she was doing cartwheels by the time we left. She needed that. I called my husband when it was over and ecstatically told him what had happened and how I had experienced a true miracle that day.

A miracle. For all the times we have to do the forgiving without getting the apology, for all the times we are not courageous enough to look our victim in the eye and apologize, I raise my peanut-butter beer and say, "Cheers to *you*, Sheldon, for being so incredibly brave and taking a risk on me. It's one I will *never* regret taking on you."

TRUST ME

Taking risks in relationships is important because we never know the profound impact they can have on a person's life. I believe what happened between Sheldon and me caused a lot of glory for God, even in the heavenly realms. I rejoiced over that reconciliation between souls for months. I know it was God who brought me to Sheldon's town and God who moved Sheldon's heart. It encouraged me, and I hope you, too, will consider taking brave risks in relationships.

What I love most about doing marriage counseling is supporting and encouraging others to take risks right in my office, to say things they may not otherwise know to say or how to say. I can often hear the subtle desperation from one partner needing to hear how valued, loved, and respected they are by the other, but they are stuck bickering about something else. Defenses melt away by the simple words of affirmation from their other half. When someone knows they are appreciated, they are willing to do and tolerate a lot more.

GET MARRIED, THEY SAID

It's the risk to our ego that makes intimate relationships so sacred. To know and be known, flaws and all, is what intimacy is all about. The opposite results in a relationship battlefield, feuding about finances and the children, alienation of affection, affairs of all kinds, and ultimately, divorce. I hear spouses begging their partner to accept them for who they are and express admiration and respect to them. It makes receiving correction more palpable because we don't hear, "You're a fuck up," when our partner suggests we not speak that way to our child. Couples must work to create an environment of acceptance, unconditional, positive regard, fierce love, and solidarity. When this foundation is in place, bickering will be short-lived, correction can be met with humility, and sarcasm can be received as friendly-fire. If there are cracks in this foundation, many conversations will be competitive, hurtful, and shut down as the other's motives are assumed to be snide and unkind. You will live as enemies.

When you allow your primary partner to be themselves, and love and regard them highly the way they are, they become empowered to grow toward their best self because someone believes in them. Suggestions or even criticisms are not characterological attacks. You understand you need to adjust your behaviors and attitudes toward another person, but that doesn't mean you, as a person, are unworthy, unlovable, or unacceptable. But if you feel fundamentally unlovable in your relationship, all comments will be received as attacks. You feel you are not good enough, so every comment builds the case against you. Defenses go up, no one exposes their true self, the environment is hostile and dangerous, and the other person is a mirror to be destroyed. It happens so quickly and insidiously, transforming that starry-eyed bride or groom into a married wife or husband who is scratching their head and wondering, *What the hell happened? I once loved this person as much as I hate them now.*

Are you in a relationship that needs to be accepted or changed? What about your significant other? Simple advice: Don't do the *changing* until the *accepted* is well-rooted. Build the foundation before picking out the curtains, so to speak. Make it your desire and mission to affirm your partner's importance and necessity in your life. Then you can start building the house brick-by-brick on that solid foundation. Otherwise, the bricks will become weapons you throw at each other, rather than a house.

TRUST GOD

People often don't take risks because of fear: fear of failure, looking a fool, or losing big. We need a deep belief in ourselves, others, and/or God to take risks. You're pretty sure it will work out, but not doomed if it doesn't. I can only presume that the richest folks may have risked big money, the happiest folks may have risked great sadness, and the successful probably have risked multiple failures. If you ever rolled the dice and wound up better off for it, congratulations! If you've failed, then chances are you learned something for the next risk, so congratulations! If you tithe, you are taking the ultimate risk with the only guaranteed win.

My husband and I began tithing (giving 10 percent of all income to God) when we first got married. We were fortunate enough to have a church with marvelous teaching at Savannah Christian Church. Our pastor never shied away from a good tithing sermon, despite the widespread misconception that churches are "after your money." The church produced several folks who gave accounts of how the Lord had blessed them financially when they began to tithe, and the pastor boldly charged his church to a ninety-day challenge to see for themselves. He even offered the suggestion of tithing to another church to prove this principle would be effective in each person's personal life, and not the life of the church-building and newly paved parking lot.

Tithing appears risky, particularly if you are working paycheck to paycheck like so many Americans. You might think, *Where on earth would I get that kind of money? I struggle to pay bills*, or maybe you have expensive hobbies, give all your money to your kids, or simply feel that you earned it, so you should keep it. And the way I see it, that's fine. You'll actually never know what you're missing out on. The blessings will never be brought to light, and you can continue along your struggle just the same. Or you can look at it differently. The first tenth of your income belongs to God, so not paying is robbing the Lord. This was reason enough for my husband and I to decide to tithe. It was clear, and we were pretty obedient, rule-following people (and by we, I mean my husband). We didn't even consider that money ours to use or give away. We only considered our spendable income to be 90 percent of what we made. Period. What we couldn't have truly foreseen was just how faithful God was to his Word. There is one time in the Bible when God tells us to test Him and see for ourselves.

"Bring the full tithe into the storehouse, that there may be food in
my house. And thereby put me to the test, says the Lord of hosts,
if I will not open the windows of heaven for you and pour down
for you a blessing until there is no more need. I will rebuke the
devourer for you, so that it will not destroy the fruits of your soil,
and your vine in the field shall not fail to bear, says the Lord of
hosts. Then all nations will call you blessed, for you will be a land
of delight, says the Lord of hosts."

— Malachi 3:10

I can tell God I love Him all day long, but when I part with "my" money for Him, I *show* Him. After all, it is a relationship. We love each other. He wants my trust, giving my first-fruits, not my left-overs. Giving what's left over is no show of faith at all. I show Him I trust Him as the maker or breaker of my life. Then He shows off for me, and my love and faith grow more. It's not a "rule," it's a principle of relationships. Give and take. God has blessed us beyond measure and can do the same for you. I would never not tithe; the peace of mind that comes from knowing God will provide all of my financial needs and even desires is priceless. And it only costs me 10 percent. This paradoxical principle works with other resources. God is able to bend time and events in our favor when we give it to Him. Don't have enough time in your life? Give some to God.

YOU LOSE

We can trust God 100 percent. People, however, not so much. The real risk is putting our faith in others. My cousin Tim was married for eight years with two children when his wife left him. He was in his late twenties, parenting his kids part-time, and paying a lofty amount of child support. That's when he met another lovely woman named Susan. She was educated, beautiful, sweet, and adored children. She had never been married, nor did she have any children of her own, but she doted on Tim's, and even mine, at family barbeques. They had been together over a year when I pulled him aside at a pool party and gushed over his new love interest. I knew he'd been lonely for a while, and I didn't think he'd find much better than this awesome girl. He was indeed proud to have found another amazing partner, one who was even more committed than his ex-wife and also, seemingly, more down to earth, but he said he would "never marry again."

I poked at him a little bit the way older siblings or cousins do. "Oh, come on! She's great! What's wrong with you?" His face dropped, he looked straight ahead, and proclaimed again, "I will never marry again." "Why, though?" "Nope, just not gonna do it. I'm committed to her. I love her, but I will never get married or have any more children, and I've made that clear to her." He couldn't explain it, really, but over time, I got to know more men who swore off marriage after the first one failed. I have come to believe that men, in particular, are brutally and morally wounded when they "fail" to keep their family together. Divorce is an ultimate failure for men. I think many of them, particularly previous Soldiers like my cousin, take their vows seriously, and when the woman leaves, they will never, ever risk that kind of failure and/or betrayal again.

Later in the hot tub, Susan and I had a woman-to-woman talk. I had really grown to like her. She was quite the sweetheart and adored and respected my cousin so much. I asked her where she thought the relationship was going? She told me Tim didn't want to get married or have any more children, and although she had always dreamed of these things, she would sacrifice them for him. "After all, he may change his mind. You never know." I wouldn't be disloyal to my cousin, but I felt obligated to speak up for women everywhere at that point. "I hope you're right. But personally, I've learned, if a man tells you who he is or who he isn't, believe him." She wasn't at the following year's barbeque.

The following year, Tim introduced me to his new, fun, and amazing lady. (He has really good taste and luck, apparently.) I hung out with them this past summer and like any good older cousin would, grilled them on their relationship. "We have never been happier with anyone else in our lives. She is my soulmate. Marriage, dear cousin? Ya never know; it just might be worth the risk of getting hurt again."

SUMMARY

Why are you here in this life? If it's to make any sort of lasting impression, you'll need to take a risk. Raise your hand when you're not sure you know the right answer. Give that guy or girl a chance at wooing your heart. Invest. Try that auburn hair color, or apply to that school, or reapply to that school, or re-reapply to that school. Move away from home. Talk about your scary childhood to a partner or therapist. Travel. If you can tolerate the worst thing you fear, then you are unstoppable. I wish I could tell you that you won't die, be abandoned, look silly, lose the farm, or fail. But God doesn't promise a smooth passage—only a safe landing.

EXERCISE

1. What do you have left to achieve? What is the worst possible outcome? How can you better tolerate this outcome? What do you need to tell yourself? What will you or others gain from achieving this mission?

———————————————————————————

———————————————————————————

_____

_____

2. Have you ever risked big and lost big? Have you ever risked big
    and won big?

    _____

    _____

    _____

    _____

Chapter 14

Organizing Your Life

"Go to sleep. I'll stay up and worry about it."

— God

The following chapter is not about managing your own life precisely so you can succeed and be your best self. It is meant to help you stay on the track the Lord has set before you. Not to be confused with the lie, "God helps those who helps themselves." God will rescue the lost over and over and over again. There is no limit to the number of chances you get from God. You just might not be living out God's will for your life by constantly straying away or sleepwalking through life, making it feel like a disappointment and a struggle. God wants us to show up in life, equipped with armor and preparedness—awake, organized, and paying attention. God has a plan.

YOUR BRAIN CANNOT BE TRUSTED

Have you ever thought to yourself, *Crap, I just remembered...*? A thought that seemingly came out of the blue popped in your head with no advance warning. Or maybe you were trying to remember something and it just wouldn't come. The answer was on the tip of your tongue, but your brain was letting you down. Ever wonder why random thoughts drift through your mind at three in the morning, or what in the name of God *that* dream was about? Or maybe you were driving your daily drive and suddenly realized you passed your exit two miles ago. Or what about when you have a visual flash in your mind that makes you puke a little when someone is telling you a story about an injury or nudity?

I was tucking my daughter in one night when she told me a story she had heard from some friends at school and the conclusion that could be made from it.

"So," she said, "these men walk into a church with loaded rifles and shout that anyone who is a Christian will be killed. Some people flee, but others stay and stand the ground of their faith. The men ultimately put down their guns and worship with the *true* Christians. The others proved their weak or nonexistent faith and were eliminated, for only those true to the Lord remained."

When she finished, I asked her what she thought about the story. She said she thought it was a happy ending. She felt that everyone got what they deserved. "Gosh," I said, "I hope my faith isn't tested that way. I'm not sure I'd pass." She looked confused because, well, she somehow views me as holier than thou. "I'm glad that God can see my heart because I'm not sure I could trust my brain to respond the way I would want to will it to. With a gun pointed in my face, I might just run and hate myself later. I don't try to react the way I do sometimes, like when I swear when I'm fired up, and it's like my responses have a mind of their own. Thank God He knows my heart and His Grace is sufficient for a scaredy-cat like me." I could see her wheels turning as we said goodnight.

We can be victims of our tricky minds that fire electrical signals pretty randomly and without our say so. For people exposed to trauma, the memories can be a living nightmare until they are able to get help from a trained therapist to process those memories and store them in a less intrusive spot in the mind. The combat veterans I've worked with often express horrible guilt over how they've fled or frozen during a life-threatening situation or how they got a boner after shooting the enemy and now can hardly live with themselves for being a monster. Please know that few biological impulses are within our control and they have absolutely nothing to do with our character.

Many confusing dilemmas of the mind are managed by writing. I've often instructed folks with intense feelings for another person, whether love or hate, to write them a letter, get it out, while encouraging them to bring it back and not give it to the person. For folks with a recurring nightmare, writing the dream out with a different ending is a way of abolishing it for good. Some folks find journaling incredibly relaxing and helpful for working through feelings. The idea is to process. Writing thoughts out into story form with a beginning, middle, and end organizes them and gives them some meaning. The result is that we can begin to feel sane again—like there is reason and meaning behind our inner turmoil—and plan a course of action. For instance, maybe you toss and turn one night. You are recounting a conversation you had earlier with a coworker. They made a comment about you not really liking your job. It bugged you for some reason. Most comments roll right off your back, but this one you've been flipping around in your head for several hours. Maybe you sit down at your computer to tell the Word document all about it. As you're writing about the day's events, you begin to tear up. Truth is, you do hate your job, but you feel stuck. You are embarrassed that someone noticed; was it that obvious? You wonder if you need to apologize and suck it up or quit. You decide to take action by talking to your mom about your options and perhaps getting some wise advice.

Writing about yourself and your life is a great way to take comfort in your skin, knowing you had a beginning, a middle, and a chance to write the ending. Will it be an inspiring story of resilience, beating the odds, and believing in yourself? Or perhaps it will be a story of defeat. You take the power of deciding the outcome into your own hands by writing your story, rather than letting it play out helplessly. You also begin disintegrating shame by owning your whole truth instead of denying it. Shame cannot exist where ownership resides. You may never be proud of some things you've done or experienced, but you don't have to be held hostage by shame. Many people have experienced awful times and admitted to terrible deeds, but the story doesn't end there. It ends at "But watch what I do now." You need only grab the autobiography of any great human with a horrid beginning to see that the story can flip at any time and produce great inspiration for the world for decades or centuries to come (*Antwone Fisher*, for you movie watchers). The Bible is also full of misfits who went down in history as tools used by God. Don't close the book on a bad chapter.

Bottom line, you have to get the stuff rolling around in there *out*. When the thought is outside of you, you can look at it and manage it; it's not inside of you, controlling you. You can take a look at it more objectively as a separate observer. You are not the thinker. You can watch the thoughts pass through or write them down and consider their value. For instance, folks who battle even the slightest form of depression and anxiety complain of intrusive thoughts all the time. They are loaded with self-doubt and sometimes complete doom and gloom. This is a voice in your head that you may notice and possibly pay attention to, but it's not yours, nor is it God's, nor is it speaking truth and love. You don't have to sit back and take it. Recognize it, perhaps identify its source, and examine the validity with a coach or counselor. Which of these thoughts are valid and should be accepted as truth and a guiding source for your future?

1. You don't have what it takes.
2. Remember that time you failed?
3. You can't compete with that.
4. They're all gonna laugh at you. (If you said that in Carrie's mom's voice, you read it just as I intended.)

If you guessed that none of these thoughts should be guiding lights, you are awesome. If you didn't, you are awesome. See how that works? Your worth doesn't depend on your performance nor my opinion.

Thoughts intervene at inopportune times; you must get it out, put it on paper, and then let it go. Suppose you had a thought in the middle of the night, *I forgot to put lunch money in my kid's school bag for tomorrow.* You can decide to chew on this for a while, hoping that your brain will remind you at a more opportune time, like in the morning before you're actually out the door. You quietly urge yourself to remember to do that. Maybe you will; maybe you won't. You remember the last time you forgot to pack lunch money. You had to leave work early and rush to the school before lunch period ended. Before long, you're bemoaning all of your responsibilities and wondering if all working parents struggle to keep it all together like you. Maybe you've bitten off more than you can chew. And down the rabbit hole you go. All the while, you should have written it on a sticky note on your nightstand and gone back to sleep.

MAKING LISTS

I'm a big proponent of writing things down. When I use terms like "sticky note" and "day planner," you may not be following me, depending on your age. If you're under forty, chances are you use your phone to keep information that you want out of your mind. This information could be to-do lists, drafts of emails or texts, or conflicting feelings. But I'm a pen and paper girl. You can set alarms on your phone these days to remind you to drink water. I embrace all things that help us to live more intently. Otherwise, we will simply "forget." This is autopilot. We drink water when we're thirsty (which research says is an indicator of already being dehydrated, so, too late), we buy milk once we've run out, we clean the fridge when the entire house stinks, we water the plants when we notice they are half-dead. We just react to our surroundings and spend a lot of time feeling anxious, overwhelmed, and out of control. Simply keeping lists and a huge bottle of water with you can offer so much peace of mind and energy.

I woke up on Monday morning, fed the rabbits, and thought, *Ick, I need to clean this cage.* Of course, it was a very inopportune time, so I let it go. The next day, same scenario. The next day, more of the same. I finally went inside and wrote in my day planner for later that evening "Clean Monty Python's shitty cage." The day planner is my life. I have it with me at most times, and I jot down thoughts like this that come to my mind all day long but I don't have the opportunity to address at that moment. It keeps me completely on track. I don't rely on my memory for anything, from the event I have in two months to clipping my fingernails. I manage the social and extracurricular lives of myself, my children, my husband, and our family as a whole in my day planner. My only major anxious thought is if I were to lose that thing. If my day planner is not around, I'll send myself an email, leave myself a voicemail, jot it down on my hand, or write it on a sticky note. This is how you keep yourself organized, on time, dependable, and on track.

Relying solely on your brain to work when you need it to is foolish. If you try to keep information in your head by thinking back to it from time to time or even meditating on it, you will spend less time in the now, living your life. When you write things down, you can disengage from your mind and get back to what's right in front of you—your life. Don't be afraid to plan out your days as much as you can and as much in advance as you can. Day planners go up to a year, so that's my only limitation. Because I like to use a pen, I keep whiteout close by for when plans change. I have each hour slotted for clients, workouts, conference calls, piano lessons, grabbing milk and eggs, telling so-and-so happy birthday, watching the Penn State game, stopping for an oil change, and so on. There are hundreds of tasks that could be done in a month's time, so lay it out for yourself! Then you can stop tossing it around in your head hoping you'll remember when you need to. Write it down. Don't wait for the feeling (or smell) to strike.

I also keep track of my menstrual cycle via my day planner. (Men, don't stop reading. I promise I'll be quick and this could help you too.) The day I get my period, I count out twenty days from then so I know when to expect the PMS. That way I can warn my husband so he can take the things I say with more grains of salt, and I feel better knowing life isn't actually as bad as it seems during that week. Knowing precisely when I'm PMS-ing alleviates a lot of self-doubt, guilt, and feeling fat, ugly, homesick, and lazy. I know to ride it out and bite my tongue more—to let my husband discipline the children and simply not rely on my own understanding of things. If you can predict your moods, you can take the necessary precautions.

NO PLAN, NO PROSPERITY

During my research on how to succeed, I learned that in 1979, there may or may not have been a Harvard MBA program study done resulting in a profound increase in income from the students who had a plan and wrote it down. It apparently looked like this:

- 84 percent of the entire class had set no goals at all
- 13 percent of the class had set written goals but had no concrete plans
- 3 percent of the class had both written goals and concrete plans

The results? Ten years later, the 13 percent of the class that had set written goals but had not created plans were making twice as much money as the 84 percent that had set no goals at all. However, the apparent kicker is that the 3 percent of the class that had both written goals and a plan were making ten times as much as the rest of the class. How cool is that? Although there is no evidence that this study actually took place, it could be true. And I believe, anyway, that goal-setting and planning to achieve said goals *is* the path to success.

Goals need to be specific. Very specific. My husband hates (justifiably) when I say I need him to nurture me more. I have just set him up for failure. I'm not sure he's heard that word before, let alone has any idea how to put it into practice. When from time to time on Saturday mornings I ask him if he could bring my coffee to me while I'm still in bed, he is a huge success. When he suggests I spend less money, I'm likely to roll my eyes and walk away. But when he sits down with me to go over the finances and asks me to think about where I can cut back specifically, I actually carry it out.

Goals need to be visual, measurable, and attainable. You can do this with concepts you want your spouse to act on as well as personal goals. Seeing is believing in the mind's eye, so you want to look at this attainable goal daily, not just flip it around in your head. An example of a bad goal is, "I want to lose weight this year." Try, "I want to lose four pounds this month," or better yet, "I want to lose one pound this week." Then plan your meals and workouts, write down every calorie you eat—or download the Weight Watchers App onto your phone—and keep a chart of your progress on a white board. You *will* be successful! "Ultimately, I want to be a clinical therapist." This journey of 1,000 miles will start with one step—calling the school for a registration packet or calling financial aid. Small steps over the next several years will lead to success. Stay the path by recording small, daily goals in your day planner.

GRATITUDE OR ATTITUDE?

Another list I'm a big proponent of is a gratitude list. If left to autopilot, I believe most of us tend to drift toward the negative. We roam around looking for evidence that people are assholes and that we are okay. We think catastrophically, and the media knows it. We are wired to look for a cause or someone to blame when things go wrong, and a lot of times, we feel unsure of ourselves. This is no way to live, but left unattended to, it's often where the brain goes. One night when I was tucking in my daughter, she began to cry, saying that no one in her class liked her, and that her life was crap. I held back many reactions that evening and chose to have compassion for her nine-year-old brain. We simply listed the things she had to be grateful for, from the most extraordinary to the most mundane. You may find that most of what you are "lacking" or resentful for is a First World problem, or that you are overlooking many blessings in your life. It takes a concerted effort to identify the things we are grateful for. We definitely take things like our health, limbs, and a roof for granted.

I've had some struggles, but never like breastfeeding an infant while sleep deprived. Maybe this was a breeze for you or those around you, and that's understandable, but for me, losing sleep, bleeding from my nipples, body "tore up from the floor up," and a crying baby was *torturous*. I remember one night in particular, I was up at three in the morning, as usual, pumping milk for the next day, watching *Little House on the Prairie*. I felt *awful*. It was the perfect night for this particular episode. Pa was away for whatever reason, so Ma was holding down the fort. There were Native Americans surrounding the house, threatening to attack. It was the middle of the night, and the kids slept while Ma was propped up in a rocking chair with a rifle, singing, eyes wide open so as not to fall asleep and be caught off guard by an invasion. I noted my warm bed with my *en suite* bathroom five feet away. My husband wasn't deployed, and there wasn't a war in my front yard. I heard a voice in my head that I assume was God. It said, "I've been throughout history and seen turmoil. This ain't it." That was all I needed to change my whole outlook on life, and I was immensely happier for it. Thank God I didn't stay in that state of lacking for years. I only needed to recognize what I had. Not a thing changed—just my perspective.

IF YOU LOVE ME, LET ME SLEEP

I saw a mattress commercial this morning claiming that the average person spends twenty-five years of their life asleep. Chances are your attitude toward sleep will dictate your response to that little marketing technique: what a waste of life, or I wish. But if you're not getting enough sleep, you're either not making it a priority or you have poor sleep hygiene. Getting sleep impedes upon precious and scarce "me time". Our lives are so hectic that we end up collapsing and spending our downtime binge-watching shows or indulging in other hobbies because we feel we deserve the rest/fun, and it feels good. The sacrifice is a great one, however, and I'd like you to reconsider the importance of getting enough sleep. Getting a new mattress may be the beginning of improving your quality of sleep, but I'm guessing many of us just aren't managing our sleep well because we just don't understand its importance. I'm really passionate about this one. Sleep deprivation can cause wars. Just like PMS, most people really underestimate its power to destroy. We accept it as a way of life—it is what it is—and we just need to deal. I say no. We don't just need to deal. The world would be a happier place if people got more rest.

A sleep-deprived surgeon or truck driver could do major, permanent damage as you can already guess. But for the rest of the population, the damage is more covert. It's happening in our brains and bodies and cells and relationships. Whole books have been written on the benefits of sleep, but I'll just talk about the few I picked to help pique your interest and, hopefully, convince you of the importance of getting enough sleep.

Based on my research on this topic, I've concluded that our brains defragment, sort of like a computer, while we are sleeping. Basically, what's happening is information, feelings, and memories are all getting filed away where they belong. When we don't allow enough time for these processes, we get stuck with feelings of bitterness, hostility, intrusive and anxious thoughts, and flashbacks. Our brains and our bodies also sweep themselves clean of toxins while we sleep. Glial cells are the nighttime housekeepers, responsible for third shift cleaning up of all the dead stuff that accumulates due to stress and illness and taking out the trash to make room for newly regenerated cells. Your body's metabolism runs more smoothly when you sleep, and then you form new pathways in your brain that let you learn and create new memories. Can you think of any better reason to sleep than you'll be thinner, smarter, and happier?

Many people consider sleep a quick zap to your battery—maybe a 40 percent charge will get you through the day. Some settle in for the whole night, allowing nothing less than a full-charge. How do you know if you have a full charge? You wake up naturally. No alarm clock needed. If you use an alarm clock, you're not going to bed early enough. You only need to google "Healthy sleep habits" for a vast array of tips on how to protect your sleep. You will learn that bed is for sleeping and sex only, and not to have caffeine after lunch and so on. What I care most about is that you take it seriously and understand just how important sleep is. I'll leave you in the capable hands of a therapist, sleep coach, or google search to get your sleep hygiene sorted out. I regularly suggest guided imagery for drifting into sleep. When the part of the brain that is following the imagery is engaged, the part that is responsible for problem solving is not. You are now free to let go. Many clients who have come to see me for sleep problems have been asleep, snoring, right on my couch within four minutes of trying guided imagery.

You can imagine, then, just how much more important sleep is for a child's growing brain and body. My children have distinctly separate, sleep-deprived personalities. Sometimes they sleep over at a friend's house with much looser rules for sleep times. I know the price I'm going to pay for the night out with basically free babysitting and that is a moody, whiny, negative, overly-sensitive, disobedient, sassy stinker—times two.

Adults are not much different in nature when we don't get enough sleep. Our family normally protects the sleep of all involved like it's the family jewels. We sleep trained like it was our family business, working slowly but surely toward a six in the evening to seven in the morning, uninterrupted sleep schedule for our babies into childhood. At seven and nine, they are in bed at seven at night and generally sleep until six. For the seventh year in a row, my girls' teachers have proclaimed that they are the happiest, smiley-est, and most joyful children. My husband and I walked out of parent-teacher conferences and looked at each other. "Sleep," my husband said. "Yep," I replied. High-five.

SUMMARY

Living on autopilot is like being held hostage by your past. You become a reactor at the whim of your mood, memories, hormones, and fears—sluggish, zoned-out, snappy. You need to tell your body and brain who's in charge and start responding more thoughtfully and intently. You do this by being rested, pausing, and writing. When we don't have those luxuries, Grace is enough.

EXERCISE

1. List five things you are grateful for.

   _____

   _____

   _____

   _____

   _____

2. Which of these First World problems do you complain or get angry about?
   - Long flight
   - Broken shoelace
   - Bad haircut
   - Rain
   - Chipped car paint
   - Mushy apple
   - Gym class cancelled
   - Football game not airing
   - Warm beer

   Can you think of some others?
3. Set a goal for this year. What can you do this week to get one step closer to it?

Chapter 15

Marriage: Whose Idea Was This?

"God's great cosmic joke on the human race was requiring that men and women live together in marriage."

— Mark Twain

I teach a segment of a premarital course with the Navy chaplain every few months. While Chaps is doing his part of the brief, I scan the room, looking at the faces eager to be one step closer to matrimony. I wonder why they are getting married. I wonder how long they will last. I wonder why the hell anyone isn't taking notes! No one who marries knows exactly what they are getting themselves into. And no matter how hard I try, I can't impress that upon anyone. Of course, I can't. It's a step of faith, outcome unknown. Faith that love will conquer all. Faith that the slow climb toward success and accomplishments has begun and won't detour. Faith that you will always be *the one*. Faith that they will always be *the one*. After sixteen years of marriage, I know one thing: I would never do it again.

YOUR MISSION, SHOULD YOU CHOOSE TO ACCEPT IT

Now, before you conclude that I'm not happily married, let me assure you that I most definitely am. I would do it all over again with the same man every single time, but looking back, I'm not inclined to do it again if *this* ended. Even if it ended successfully. (Meaning, someone dies. It's the only way to count a marriage a success.) Melding your life with another is one of many sacrifices and compromises, requiring lots of bending, pruning, worrying, forgiving, humbling, and intensifying. I married near age thirty, so maybe I was more set in my ways, making the adjustment harder, but it was agonizing for me. And not because my husband is hard to love, but because I was tormented by the damage done by previous relationships. Everyone and anyone will experience challenges to some degree. Make a decision to get and stay married because it will grow you in ways you wouldn't have grown otherwise; don't do it to be blissful the rest of your life. Happiness will come—and go. It's a project you work on for decades, God willing. Sound romantic? Hallmark didn't think so either.

Like any big project you will undertake, you should prepare, plan, and pray. This may mean doing workbooks together, doing date nights, or doing counseling. Just *do*. *Being* is not enough to keep the relationship functioning and intact. When my husband deployed for the first time, I was told, "Deployment makes strong marriages stronger and weak marriages weaker." Fact is, you have to be even more intentional with your thoughts and actions while apart or you will drift and become strangers. The same can happen just as easily when you see each other every day. My husband was a company commander during his year in combat and still managed to snail-mail 365 letters (some just one or two sentences) while he was away. And this was during a time of email! He simply found it more romantic, traditional, and intentional. I planned out care packages and planned our ever-anticipated reunions. I minded the house and yard and my body in a way that would make him proud. We put effort into the marriage despite the miles. While he bravely defended our country, I used the time to get back in touch with myself and grow as an individual, so I could be a better mate. I advanced my career, took art classes, learned to ride a motorcycle, studied the Bible, learned to be a better friend, explored the region, and went on a diet. Enriching yourself enriches the relationship. Keep striving to be a person of interest. It is a loving effort to put into your relationship.

THE BOOK OF MARRIAGE

A marriage goes through stages, or various chapters. In this section, I'm going to discuss the three chapters my marriage has undergone, realizing there will be many more chapters yet to come.

Chapter 1: The Corrective Experience

The first five years of my marriage were exhausting, the next five were confusing, and last five have been interesting. The first five years I spent pushing him away and looking for evidence that he was a no-good cheater. This is what I learned in my previous relationships—they end, and they end badly. There will be lots of drama, lots of betrayal, crying, and heartbreak. I was convinced he didn't love me as much as he said he did, or he wouldn't if he got to know me better. Every critique of the way I did something was proof that he thought I was worthless and "I'll fucking show you. I'm leaving *you*." I can't count how many times I packed my bags. All I know is that the number equals the number of times he wouldn't let me leave and fought me until we worked through it.

I call this chapter of marriage the corrective experience because it's where we can heal from our past by playing out old hurts and experiencing a different outcome, one of commitment, loyalty, compassion, and reassurance from the other person. You can begin to unbecome whom you learned to be in previous relationships or an unhealthy marriage and become who you were meant to be. Trust shouldn't be expected early in a relationship. I hear many couples who believe they are entitled to trust. If you were given that freely, cherish it. If not, it will build with *consistent behavior over time.*

You are perhaps partnering with or are someone with negative relational experiences in the past. Partnerships need significant support from an outside source in the beginning to help you look objectively at your reactions. I recommend you always get this support from someone who loves you both or doesn't love either of you. I know exactly which of my best girlfriends would support me with an emphatic, "Fuck him!" if I went to them with my marital gripes. They would have encouraged me to do what's best for Karen in their minds because they love me. A marriage needs someone who loves your *marriage.* If you have a healthy mother-in-law, she may be a good option for airing your grievances. A healthy woman will support you through the loving eyes of her son's mama. She will support healing and courage for you both to make amends. Make sure she's healthy. And by no means air your grievances on social media. People make the boldest comments behind their screens.

If you don't know a healthy person who supports your marriage and loves you both, or you don't want to tell said person your business, a marriage therapist or relationship coach is the way to go. Be warned: If a therapist suggests you should probably get divorced, and the situation at home is not abusive, get a second, professional opinion. Therapists are only human and get burned out. They may feel helpless and exacerbated. I feel like if you're coming to therapy, you are desperate to work through the conflict and get to a better place. My job is to be with you, one foot inside your hell and the other in the land of hope. I will stand there as long as you are willing to or until your insurance stops paying. Just kidding. I will not propose divorce unless someone in the dyad is in danger or change seems unlikely because of personality or characterological deficit. While there are many experts on marriage, John Gottman is like the Godfather. I would encourage you to know what the experts know based on longitudinal studies. Gottman can actually predict marriage failure at a greater than 90 percent success rate, making marriage success a science, in my mind.

Not only can you read a billion books on maintaining marital satisfaction, but you can have an outside source help you sort out your specific reactional patterns in the relationship and challenge the current need for those reactions. A therapist can also often help you express these needs and receive and respond to another's expression of needs. You don't necessarily have to go with your spouse to get help bringing things into focus. I had a therapist I would call on in those special moments of losing my shit because of some perceived slight by my spouse that left me spinning. She was always able to help me feel normal, and more importantly, explain the normalcy of the dance we were doing. She encouraged me to be still and watch the dance change. And it did. Therapists have a way of seeing a process that you are in and cannot see. They can educate you on how gender differences create this amazing shit show in a marriage and help you determine the reason you react the way you do and challenge these long-held beliefs. If the road is divorce-bound, a therapist can help you both navigate this process with the least collateral damage possible. You don't have to struggle alone!

Chapter 2: The Friendship Challenge

The second five years of marriage, I wondered if I would ever make this man my friend. You see, I didn't marry my best friend. I married my Prince Charming. We had passion, interesting conversation, and similar goals, values, beliefs, and ambitions. But I struggled to get past what was lacking. I would think, *Some couples sure do seem to have great friendships with their partners.* I would begrudge him that incapability for years rather than cling to the truth that he was hard-working, making all of my dreams come true, and handsome as hell. He gave me anything I wanted, including travel, while helping with the children wherever he could, yet I would dwell on the fact that he wouldn't let me crank the radio up, high-five me, or enthusiastically play board games with me and my friends.

My husband is uber-responsible and super-mature. When we met, I was suspicious of the three-year difference between us. His response was that he was the "oldest twenty-five-year-old" I'd ever met. And he was right! He didn't see the thrill in being loud, drunk, irresponsible, or spontaneous. "Mr. Fun Buster" is how I non-affectionately referred to him, taking his precautions and planning at every turn. I wondered if we just weren't right for each other while he was intensely focused on building a life of shared experiences and security. Why do we always focus on what's *missing* rather than on what we have? It's human nature, but it makes us miserable and leaves us always feeling a sense of lack. I see many couples who also become deluded by the idea that their mate should be like their best friend, a buddy. I actually don't want barstool guy who burps and chugs beer and says inappropriate things as my man. I mean, I love that guy. He is carefree like me. But at the end of the day, I'll take my courageous, honorable, loyal, smells-good, handsome, fuddy-duddy.

EXERCISE

Make a list of things you admire and respect about your partner. Then cling to those and show your appreciation for those attributes. A lot of your happiness depends on getting this perspective straightened out.

Developing a friendship would be and remains an endeavor for us. We married as acquaintances, so I don't think we're doing too badly. He's never going to tear up the dance floor with me, and I'm never going to think through everything I say and do before I say or do it. But boy, we sure did try for a long time to beat each other into the mold we wanted. We need to accept things about our partner as truth and ask for what we need without controlling them or demanding they be something different.

For instance, your roommate may never walk into a kitchen and notice dried spaghetti sauce on the counter. No matter how much you fume inside or mutter under your breath, they are never ever going to notice it. It doesn't show up on their radar. How can you control that? Humiliate, shame, coerce? That's just too exhausting, unloving, and futile. The sooner we learn to accept that, the better our mental state. If you had a love of cars and a McLaren Senna passed by, can you fault the person riding with you for not noticing? We all have different lenses we are looking through, and if you notice the overflowing trash every time, you're probably going to be the only one who cares enough about it to take it out. You can delegate this chore, but you can never make someone notice all of the same things you do.

Chapter 3: This, Too, Shall Pass

The third five years of marriage have shown me that chapters really do come and go. You can only see this truth, like many others, in the rearview mirror. You can never see it while you're in it. The two years while my husband was in command were two of the hardest for us. We would struggle daily with the stress of "getting it right." Command was an aspiration we had set our eyes on since we met. It would take a team effort more than ever to be successful and fill the shoes of previous command couples. I had to fly from England to Kansas without my children to take a weeklong class about my role as a senior Spouse and what was expected of me. Then, when we arrived at our duty station, the General's wife called me and talked at me for thirty minutes about her expectations of me. There were fellow Spouses I couldn't please no matter what I did. I felt like a burden and tried to stay out of my husband's hair so he could focus on the mission. I was working full-time after a seven-year sabbatical and parenting two small children, one of whom was struggling in school. That is how I ended up on Prozac.

My husband had his own pressures. When he's stressed, he's more vigilant; he becomes a micro-manager at home, he is less tolerant, he's serious *all* the time, and he mentally checks out when he has down time. Stress makes people go into coping mode. How we cope should not be confused with who we *are*. There were times I thought I hated my husband, but I really only hated the way he coped with stress and anxiety. I did everything I could to stay out of his way and keep the kids out of his way, increasing my own burden. I felt like the less mental and physical space we took from him, the more he could focus on this important mission and career dream. Long story short, when command was over, I got my husband back, and I think, vice versa. Just like many people, particularly those in the helping professions and all ranks of the military, you bring shit home. You can't help it. Switching gears takes time. Sometimes it happens during the commute home; sometimes it takes longer.

Improve the relationship by altering your responses. Don't take things personally, and give your mate the benefit of the doubt. They may have to tell you what they need when they walk through the door. Sometimes it's a hug or a smiling face; sometimes it's thirty minutes of space. Sometimes life will seem all about you; sometimes it will seem all about them. Don't mistake someone's coping with their character. And definitely don't close a book on a bad chapter.

SUMMARY

When I ask my husband if he would ever marry again if I die to-morrow, his response is, "Yes, but for money. I got married for love the first time, and I won't make that mistake again." We laugh because we know the electricity between us left us with no choice but to go down that road with each other and face all the practical matters that would arise. And I know he actually doesn't regret it for a minute.

Chapter 16

Giving and Receiving Grace, Mercy, and Forgiveness

"Because they know the name of what I am looking for, they
think they know what I am looking for."

— Antonio Porchia

The apostle Paul spent his life preaching the gospel that, "Christ is
the end of the law." We will now be judged by our hearts and ability to love and find forgiveness, rather than precisely carrying out
rules and blood offerings in order to be righteous before God. Paul
also told us, "Don't get married," (1 Corinthians 7:8; 7:24, 27) and
"Mind your own business" (1 Thessalonians 4:11-12). I think what
Paul knew was all the ways our disturbed hearts could be tested in
relationships. That relationships are crazy-making. That we are, at
the very core, judgmental, jealous, greedy, selfish, and insecure. It's a
lot easier to model the heart of Jesus in solitude. I'm quite lovely and
kind and patient when I'm by myself. Relationships are where we are
forced to deal with our true nature. But we are wired to need human
contact. We all want to be loved and *gotten*. We end up in relationships by birth and by choice. Some work well; some are challenging.
Truth is, all relationships (marriage, friendships, siblings, parent/
child, neighbors, coworkers) are doomed without proper care.

THE PROBLEM WITH PEOPLE

I probably don't need to tell you what's hard about accepting others' behaviors, forgiving a wrongdoing, letting go of a grudge, being kind to someone who doesn't deserve it, or biting your tongue when you're right. Chances are you have a relationship or two in your life that has exposed this ugly truth about you: You're an egotistical, record keeper of wrongs, who is also lustful, bitchy, mean, bossy, and, at times, a moody SOB. Our ego seeks to be right and separate. The bigger the ego, the more we defend it, and the more we need enemies to support it. It thrives on separateness from others. It never backs down from a fight. It looks down on others to survive. It craves importance and praise. Dying to self, or ego, is a daily struggle toward becoming more Christ-like. And relationships make it harder.

Kay came to me feeling hurt in a good friendship with Stan. He was her closest confidant, and she relied on him for emotional support when her ex-husband rained down his hatred and accusations on her. One night, Kay and Stan went out for dinner where she explained to him the recent confrontation she'd had with her ex in which he had brought up years of resentments and accusations that were not true. She was deeply hurt and needed some sympathy. After she told Stan about the wild accusations, he chuckled. She felt more wounded and shot back, "It isn't funny." "I didn't say it was funny." "But you laughed and it felt like you were minimizing how awful this was for me." "I laughed! That doesn't mean I thought it was funny. I don't appreciate being accused of something I didn't do. Do you want to tell me what else I do that you can't stand about me?"

See what happened there? People respond based on the lenses they are looking through and the experiences they've had. That's the ego at work. It is defending and protecting itself at all times, even when a friend needs you to be "without self" for few moments. The more trauma one has had in life, the more protective one becomes. We go through life watching, waiting, and looking for evidence that we are, for lack of a better word, unlovable. We all do it to some degree. Some people are better at managing their external reactions, denying the self, and giving grace and mercy to others. My childhood friend, Barbara, messaged me out of the blue the other day, making me aware of a Facebook conversation between her and another friend of mine. Her message to me was very accusatory because I had "let" the other friend name-call her in his comment on my thread. (You with me?) I hadn't even seen this conversation, so I went to look for it. They had words, and I sort of felt bad for both of them. However, she was irate with me for not coming to her defense, stating that I "clearly lacked loyalty." Being the asshole I am, I defended myself by calling their little repartee immature and mutually offensive. Basically, my ego wasn't going to let her get away with undermining my good intentions and virtues.

Much later, I'm sorry to say, I was reminded of some childhood trauma I knew she had experienced. The name-calling on his part was particularly offensive about her looks, which I knew she was insecure about. She needed her best friend to show up on the "Facebook playground" and put turd-face in his place. A deep sadness fell over me. A sadness for the little girl version of Barbara who had been hurt and sad and for my own scrappy inner child who had let her down. It made sense, and while I could have stood my ground and gained support, I could eventually get past it all and see the hurt—the hurt that wrecks relationships. We had managed to come this far without a severe altercation, and just like that, I felt a break that could very well be irreconcilable.

All relationships totter on the edge of doom. People should come with warning labels, "If you get too close, you will be hurt or disappointed by me at some point." Sometimes I'm tired and quiet—aloof. This will feel like a slight, and you will wonder if it's personal or if I'm simply rude. Sometimes you will be right. Sometimes I will be in a hurry and get straight to the point without any niceties. You will wonder if I'm mad at you or just a downright bitch. Sometimes, I will be one or the other or both. And sometimes my anxiety will kick in, and I will act like I'm better than you. I'm a liar.

HURT PEOPLE HURT PEOPLE; HEALED PEOPLE HEAL PEOPLE

You never really know someone. I don't care if you grew up in the same household, with the same parents, or lived together for fifty years. Everyone creates their own personal narrative of what is happening around them, and there is no right or wrong—just that person's truth. And before we judge the truth that they tell themselves, we should know that it depends largely on infant experiences, possibly womb experiences, genetics, transgenerational trauma, and many other environmental factors. These truths are carried through life by people constantly scanning their surroundings, judging others, and validating their truths. It happens out of our conscious awareness by means of maintaining an attitude or belief about life events based on experiences. These *implicit attitudes* can lead to behaviors that lend themselves to *self-fulfilling prophecies*. (Example: I believe people don't like me, so I act shitty so that they don't, and then I'm right.) We figuratively stack the deck in favor of our assumption of others with *confirmation bias* where we scan for evidence that our belief is accurate (i.e., See, I was right). Our perception keeps us from seeing others' true intentions; rather we are skeptical of others' goodness or even badness. Sound confusing? It is! The intricate inner, unconscious workings of an individual are way beyond your or my realm of understanding. Everyone sees things through a unique lens.

"The heart is deceitful above all things and beyond cure. Who can understand it?"

— Jeremiah 17:9

"Trust in the Lord with all your heart and lean not on your own understanding."

— Proverbs 3: 5-6

The experiences that affect our actions and reactions most powerfully are the traumatic ones. Some experiences keep us on the defensive, and when triggered, they put us straight into fight-or-flight mode. It doesn't have to be an actual threat (you thought your words were harmless, so the other person is ridiculous for taking them so personally). It doesn't have to make sense, and it only needs to *feel* similar to the original injury. We survive by being vigilant of others, trying to make sense of the world, gaining a sense of control, and building a sense of self. That's a lot at stake.

I once had a woman shush me in a meeting. I was having a sidebar conversation with another woman to clarify my role. Whatever it was that triggered her, I do not know. But I lost my shit. At the end of the meeting, I leaned down to her eye level and said, "Don't ever fucking 'shush' me again." She was reduced to tears, and my ego was well satisfied—I had defended the little girl in me or whatever the hell was going on. It wasn't long before I felt the Holy Spirit convicting me for my intimidating ways.

"Therefore, as God's chosen people, holy and dearly loved, clothe yourselves with compassion, kindness, humility, gentleness, and patience."

— Colossians 3:12

"Clothe yourselves." Not "Conjure it up from inside." This to me means, "Act as if," because you don't have it in you. At least not all the time. People lash out when they are triggered, myself included. I'm fortunate to have therapists as friends and a God who won't leave me in that sorry state. The tough lovers of the world believe that some behavior is inexcusable, that everybody makes choices based on the exact same freedom and mental wellbeing, and that God, "helps those who help themselves." Thank God for not being like that. There are far too many opportunities to be broken to think God expects perfect behavior. Men without mothers, daughters without dads, depressed parents, inappropriate grandparents, bullying siblings. But God ultimately want us to heal. The more healed we are, the more drama-free our relationships can be. I come across the following from time to time on Facebook, and it cracks me up every time:

A first date question:

"How aware are you of your traumas and suppressed emotions, and how are you actively working to heal them before you try to project that shit on me?"

Truth!

How do you keep family and friend relationships from going haywire? Let's now discuss a few methods to help you keep your cool when dealing with others.

DETACHED ATTACHMENT

One of the stinkiest things about people is our inability to love unconditionally. Or maybe we think we love unconditionally, but liking and accepting and supporting unconditionally is a different story. I lost a very important relationship when I failed to break up with a boyfriend who told constant lies. I was in love and didn't know I could do any better, and my friend disapproved. We didn't speak for three years, until the relationship with liar-boy finally ended. She would probably say she loved me during that estrangement, but couldn't bear my choices or how self-deprecating I was being in settling for his crap. I think she felt that if she remained in a relationship with me, it would mean she was condoning what I was doing. And though it wasn't immoral, illegal, or unethical, she couldn't stand by and watch, I suppose. I get that, because I've been on her end too.

Another friend was broken-hearted and behaving in ways I felt were demeaning to her—ways that I had already judged my younger-self harshly for. People do whatever they can to heal, feel okay, and powerful and in control again. Because we were so close, I felt a personal attachment and responsibility to her pain and helping her cope with it. I so wanted her to respond to the creep who had dumped her with a big "FU," but instead, she blamed herself and tried to be more attractive in an attempt to win him back. She would get glimmers of hope that he wanted her back, and her mood would change entirely from bitchy to cheerful. She acted like an incredibly hurt person—needy, desperate, and in my mind, pathetic. It wouldn't be long until I got so angry with her that I began to distance myself from her, and ultimately, our friendship ended. I really did want to support her through the breakup and see her heal. For me, that meant her growing a backbone and nothing else. I labeled her actions weak and thought she was letting me down. I couldn't listen to it anymore. I couldn't tolerate the irrational beliefs of a broken-hearted, deeply wounded woman who was harshly rejected from what she believed was her destiny. I got angry at her ex when she wouldn't. Because I couldn't make her see what I wanted her to see, I couldn't stand to be in the relationship anymore.

With a healthier mindset, I would have shown compassion and support independent of how she healed. My best friend not talking to me during my relationship with a creep years ago now started to make sense. If you want someone to behave differently, you have to set boundaries or have some guts, but the other person needs to go through the lesson themselves. You can't tell someone when they've *had enough*. Only the person enduring the heartache knows when they've had enough. Close, loyal friends find it tough to be detached cheerleaders because they believe friends "take your lickin's with you." Sometimes our friends are on a bit of a roller-coaster ride in life, and we can stay down on solid ground and cheer them through it, or we can get on it with them. If we do, we risk getting sick and puking all over them.

What hurts you, hurts me. It's hard to watch. But one of my biggest life lessons as a therapist and friend is that you can't tell people their truth. They have to find it for themselves. In the end of *The Wizard of Oz*, Glinda the Good Witch offers to send Dorothy back to Kansas after her long and tiring journey trying to find her own way back home. One of her companions on the journey then asks Glinda why she didn't tell Dorothy how to get back home right from the start. Glinda responds, "Because she wouldn't have believed me. She had to learn it for herself." Stay off people's roller coasters and let them it ride out, for as long as they need to, maintaining your stable footing.

I've seen people stop talking to a parent because they started smoking again or were getting a divorce. We don't always understand others' actions, and when we think we know better or disapprove, our loved one gets left out in the cold. The tough-lovers of the world have little grace for messy people. What if we could love someone with all the support and dignity they deserve and the grace and mercy that's been given to us? That's easier to do in a detached relationship. Intimacy is in dire need of grace and mercy to survive. We need more "you do you"—today's expression of grace and mercy. It's how we try to accept people where they are, coping with their stuff however they can, based on where they've been and where they hope to be.

How does our trying to decide if they deserve our affection and doling it out accordingly help? It's about providing love and care to others without becoming emotionally involved in what they are doing. This is detached attachment. It's depending on your own peace and happiness; therefore, placing no conditions on how others act or choose to receive your love.

Detached attachment should not be confused with keeping a safe distance from others. I am a huge supporter of friend-timacy and closeness. But without the appropriate boundaries, these close friendships can be unhealthy because the relationship can be tiring and lead to compassion fatigue, lashing out in order to gain some distance, and experiencing detraction from your other important relationships.

How do we keep healthy boundaries? We start by recognizing when our feelings begin changing our behavior toward a loved one—we have difficulty practicing kindness and offering loving advice when asked to support their hopes and dreams. For me, I knew it meant praying incessantly for my friend's ex to return to her (if it was God's will) and keeping my mouth shut unless she was doing something unsafe. It would mean focusing on other relationships, letting God be God in her life, and taking care of myself. It meant owning my own peace of mind and happiness, rather than postponing those joys until she came around and did what I thought she should do. It's the kind of care I am able to provide when I'm not really invested in the person or the outcome. When friendships or family relationships get deep and involved, they are doomed without grace and mercy to keep them from meeting their demise. Fortunately, forgiveness can heal a broken relationship.

FORGIVENESS

When I got married, I was given all kinds of advice, but what stuck with me was, "The key to a good marriage is short-term memory loss." Forgiveness has been debated and struggled over for centuries. It's often what brings folks in to counseling—they are trying to bridge the canyon, the void between *wanting to get over it* and *getting over it*—actually letting someone off the hook. Definitions have been perfected over the decades, and the modern notion of forgiveness is that it is a gift to yourself, not the other person. It's letting yourself off the hook. I think the definition varies from case to case. Sometimes it's choosing to let hurts bounce off you because you have compassion for what's happening beneath the surface. Sometimes it's simply choosing not to remember over and over every day. Somedays it means, "I think about it every day; I just won't seek revenge or punishment." And my favorite:

> *"Forgiveness means I no longer dwell on what an asshole you are. You're still an asshole."*
>
> — *Unknown*

What about forgiveness of self? In my research, I discovered zero mention of self-forgiveness in the Bible! Jesus talked a ton about things that still really matter to us today (rest, money, hell), but never once about forgiving one's self. I think that in achieving joy, it is paramount that we know we are off the hook. We are not off the hook due to anything we did, but because Jesus hung on a cross. You are off the hook, like it or not. I have a buddy in New Zealand who was visiting Hawaii, and during a hike, somehow the topic of owing people came up. "Oh, I will not owe anyone! That's the worst!" he said. Everyone on the hike gave a robust show of agreement. It made me realize why people struggle with receiving forgiveness. No matter how heinous the crime, Jesus offers forgiveness, freely, to anyone who simply asks. He knows, "They know not what they are doing" (Luke 23:34).

THINK LIKE A THERAPIST

No one is more objective at helping you with your personal mess than a therapist. We therapists are trained to stay off your roller-coaster and provide you with the kind of relationship that will help you *grow*. We believe people are responsible for and completely in charge of their own lives. We believe people are basically good and strong, and if they have someone in their life who believes in them and accepts them unconditionally, they will figure out their own shit and be receptive to some guidance. We expect people to fall back into old behaviors and coping, even when they've shown signs of change, before they finally make progress. We know that no matter how much we know and how clearly we see the situation, there are factors that we don't know, and we have no right to determine anyone's fate or decide what the right choice is for them. We know that, given the circumstances of their lives, people are doing the best they possibly can at the moment. People are enigmas—being curious and intrigued is respectful. Thinking you know anything about someone is not. If my emotions didn't blind me, I could be this person to my loved ones. But often, I can't.

SUMMARY

We either cave in to shame or look down on others. But I believe anyone is capable of any sin given the wrong circumstances and timing. With this in mind, we are all connected by having the same potential for a major fall. Some just didn't start out with the same possibilities or momentum. I also believe that people need to believe what they need to believe to sleep at night. That may mean you will always be the bad guy in some people's eyes. I say this so that you might examine your ability to give grace and mercy. Often, we want to be God and decide who is worthy and who is not. We usurp God when we judge others, not knowing anything about their upbringings, experiences, traumas, or genetics.

The Bible has nothing to say on the topic of self-forgiveness. I don't think it's required of us. What's available to us, though, is the opportunity to receive it from the Judge Himself! You don't have to conjure up a merciful attitude with yourself from inside. Sometimes it's too huge a task for us. All we have to do is receive and accept this freely given gift. If you are successful at giving others grace, mercy, and forgiveness, and receiving it from the Source, then you can find joy and give joy in your relationships with others. Then the relationships that your heart and soul so desperately desire can soar!

EXERCISE

1. Whom do you need to stop harboring resentment toward, simply because you don't have all the facts?

    _____

    _____

    _____

    _____

    _____

2. What do you need to receive forgiveness for once and for all?

_____

_____

_____

_____

_____

Chapter 17

Being the Best Version of Yourself

"If you're pretty, you're pretty; but the only way
to be beautiful is to be loving. Otherwise, it's just
'Congratulations about your face.'"

— John Mayer

You were made for more. Possibly more than you could ever imagine. Plans for us unfold when we stay close to God. I think many people think of God as someone who rewards good behavior and punishes bad and has a presence like human authority—folded arms, wagging finger—trying to keep us in line and stop us from having fun. We are told God helps those who help themselves and is a distant ruler, judging from on high. In fact, God says, "If you will obey me and keep my covenant, you will be my own special treasure from among all the peoples on earth." Special treasure? That sounds like how I think about my children. They are my pride and joy. I love and *adore* seeing them happy and pleased and praised and spoiled by their aunties. But if you think I could possibly love my children more than God loves us, you'd be way off.

I think you can have a close relationship with God by just being who you are (not perfect, thank you, Jesus). The closer your walk with God, the closer you get to becoming your best. What does that look like? God plans to prosper us (Jeremiah 29:11). I would never try to predict what that looks like for you or anyone else. My sister serves the Lord, and finding her fulfillment meant a major downsizing of her home and most of her belongings. Prosperity means to have a fulfilling and rich life, whatever that means for you. That is a promise that's between you and God.

And it's a promise you can claim. Do you have any part in the relationship? Yes! Does it mean getting as close to perfection as you can before asking God to look and listen to us? No! God is easy to please, but hard to satisfy. Christ delights in your feeble attempts to please Him, but He will always compel you toward more, just as we applaud our babies on their first few steps long before we're done teaching them how to walk. Jesus was the ultimate blood sacrifice, making it possible for us to go before God every day just as we are and be approved of regardless. Our part, once we fully embrace that offer, is to seek, praise, and honor Him. It's the only natural response once you've fully grasped what God did (John 3:16).

SEEKING

My friend asked me once, "How do we *really* know God is all He says He is?" God promises "Seek and you shall find" (Matthew 7:7). What does that look like? Again, I can't tell you what that would look like for you. I believe when you seek God, what you find will be a God unique to you. No one else could know or understand or maybe even believe based on your experience. God gets that intimate with us. God is not above playing a song on a secular radio station at just the right time to let you know He is there and cares for you. Whatever it is, *you'll* know.

Do yourself a favor and follow the Leader, not the followers. Don't seek the Lord by sitting at the feet of other Christians and letting them tell you what it should look like. I had a client once who was raised in a Christian cult. He was an adult with his own family when he came to me because he had come to see how disturbing some of the beliefs held by the group were. He was having a hard time trusting God because of the lies he'd been told growing up. He was seeking answers from me and anyone else who would steer him in the right direction. Problem was, he was following the followers—then and now: the imperfect, sometimes confused, and faulty followers. He needed to go right to the Source and ask God to walk with him in truth and light, opening his eyes to what is real. If you've ever been turned off by Christianity because of *so and so*, you aren't following the Leader; you're following the follower.

My daughter and I were reading about the Crusades last night. That's what happens when she tells me she has a book report due in three days and hasn't started the book yet—we read together, taking turns. The book focused on modern Turkey and revisited some of the history that led to the current religious climate in Turkey. The book explained that the Apostle Paul preached in the area, organizing the first Christian church. Christianity would later be declared the official religion of that region by the Roman Emperor Constantine. Somewhere along the way, Christians became murderers, so they remain hated by the majority there to this day. My daughter put the book down and with a very concerned look asked, "Mama, what happened? How could that happen?"

"Well, humans do what humans do. They form groups, separating themselves from the 'others,' and well, only one group can be 'right.' You'll see this happen in school," I told her. "People will break into groups with others who are 'like' them and anyone else is wrong and on the outside. Christianity was never meant to be a club, but a change of heart. That's what went wrong."

PRAISING

Before accepting Jesus as her Savior, my friend asked me, "Why does God 'need' us to worship Him. I mean, isn't that a little narcissistic? 'Worship me!'?" God doesn't need our worship, *we* need to worship. We are all wired to worship something, and we will. It may be ourselves, another person, things, or maybe money. It's whatever gratifies the ego, makes 'something of yourself,' makes you stand out among others, or makes you feel good enough or better than. If God is Love, and all that is pure, holy, wise, and powerful, is that not what we should adore and set our sights on? All that is good and perfect? Or does nature deserve our praise and worship? Maybe a professional ball player does? Maybe our kids do? Anything you put before your love of God is an idol. We are warned against idols simply because they are imperfect, impure, fallible, and temporary. Imagine if the whole world worshipped Love, Truth, and all that is good and pure!

To me, praise is not something I give freely because I think it should be reserved for excellence. God gets my praise because He is Worthy. I don't gush over people and their accomplishments the same way I would proclaim all that God has done. Setting Him apart from others and showing Him that I value Him more than anything else is my way of communicating my love for Him and acknowledging His love for me. I don't clap for the pastor when he comes on stage or for the band when worship is over. I've gone to some massive and very entertaining light-show churches with mind-blowing preaching. I want it to be clear to God Whom I'm there to see and give my credit and admiration to. Have you ever seen someone given credit for something they didn't do? One of the biggest misconceptions I see so widely spread is that of "The Paradoxical Commandments," often referred to as the poem "Anyway," being written by Mother Teresa. In fact, many copies of this poem are sold in stores, framed, and credited to her. Truth is, the author of this popular poem is Dr. Kent M. Keith. Mother Teresa thought the poem was important enough to put on the wall of her orphanage in Calcutta, and the rest is history. I wince every time I see this poem rotated around social media with Mother Teresa as the credited author. I'm not saying she deserves no glory or admiration. But not in this case. All perfect gifts come from Him (James 1:17). Let's give credit where credit is due.

Along these same lines, I have friends whom I believe consider Jesus the Way, the Truth, and the Life, yet depend on other sources (maybe, just in case?) for confirmation. That is no worship at all. You either put your trust in someone or you don't. Half-hearted trust is not trust. That's like saying there are multiple truths. That's an oxymoron. There is only one truth. You can't say "Everyone is right." That's not true. Everyone has a different perspective, but there is only one truth. One day, everyone will know it. Just the same with trust. You either do or you don't. You don't get on a plane and pray that it won't crash as well as cross your fingers! Pick one thing to believe in and give it your full faith. I don't let my children throw money in fountains because it promotes two things: carelessness with money and putting your faith in a fountain. I know cultures that flip cups upside down when something has been lost or gone missing. It's just a cute, harmless ancestral tradition. Or is it? I think it's a show of distrust or partial trust in the Lord: that He's not always paying attention or doesn't care enough to help us find what we need. He wants to be your *only* Source of help. I think it's insulting to your relationship with God to trust Him and a cup "just in case." That's not trust. That's half-assed faith. Worship is giving all your faith and credit to the One who deserves it.

HONORING

When you love someone, you honor them. I wasn't raised in a strict home, but two things I remember my mom being adamant about were you do not take the Lord's name in vain, and you don't wear crosses as jewelry. "The cross is not a fashion-statement," she would say. She was teaching me about reverence and taking my relationships seriously. When she caught me smoking at sixteen, she barely protested, but my sister and I knew never, ever to diminish our Lord in our words or actions.

When I married my husband, he had certain rules that he lived by as a bachelor, just as I did. One of his super-annoying chores was always to shred his name and address on all mail that he received so he could recycle the piece of mail. This required ripping the address out of every single piece of mail, junk and all (envelope and inner contents), and shredding each one, every day. Then, recycling the paper that went into a different receptacle than the trash. When I was a single gal, all that crap went in the trash. Period. I wouldn't even open the obvious junk, just pitch it. I like to keep my life simple and organized, and throwing away mail was an easy way to keep myself sane. Now I had to open every piece of mail, look for and rip out anything with our name, address, account number, etc. on it and shred each piece? I did it because I hated being nagged about not doing it, and why the hell not? In the grand scheme of things, it was that important to him to do things safely, methodically, and by the book.

The true *test* of my honor as a wife was during year-long deployments. I was free. I could live however I wanted. Do whatever I wanted. Hot damn! I was gonna toss all the mail in the garbage and think about more important things. Problem was, my husband felt really strongly about this. *But he'd never know.* I really loved him, and it was important to him. *But he'd never know.* I felt my independent, and quite frankly, rebellious heart urging me on my own way, my own terms, making my own happiness and survival of greater importance than doing what I knew he'd want for our household. Crap. I was looking at another year of opening and shredding and opening and shredding. Not out of guilt. I had every right to make my life as simple as I needed to. But between honor or convenience, the choice for me was obvious.

You obey out of trust and honor out of love. If God created you and wants the best for you, and He knows the past, present, and future, it's only natural to obey Him. But as a culture, we struggle with that word. Our search is to be self-sufficient and do things our way. Personally, I'd rather be told what to do by the only One who knows what the heck is going on. And I love how He blesses me when I do. It's not that He rewards our good behavior (that's not really a relationship). But it is a mutual experience. We take steps of faith; He gives us solid footing. We ask; He answers. We obey Him; He treasures us. We try; His Grace goes the rest of the way.

BEHAVE AS THOUGH

Last week, I did something I really didn't want to do. It was my husband's birthday and we wound up at his favorite burger joint indulging in dollar PBRs (Pabst Blue Ribbon beer); we are that classy. My eager seven-year-old thought we should make some sort of fuss about Daddy's birthday, so naturally, I attempted to pawn it off on the waitress by mentioning the fact that it was his birthday when we ordered. She smiled and walked away. Apparently, there was going to be no fuss, no free ice cream, and no singing from the staff. I was comfortable with that; my seven-year-old was not. She wasn't letting me off the hook. "Mommy," she whispered, "I want everyone to sing to Daddy." When I replied, "I told the waitress, honey, but I guess they don't do that here," she was not pacified.

I didn't know whether it was God, mom guilt, or shame because I had just written the chapter about the gift of enthusiasm, but I was being strongly compelled to invite the entire restaurant to join me in singing to my husband. I scanned the room to decide if I had the nerve to follow my conviction. I saw about seventy bikers on the patio, the dining room held six families, and there were a few men at the bar. So, no. Nope. No way. Not going to happen. I hadn't even finished my first beer. *I'm not doing this, God. Please, please, please let me off the hook,* I prayed. My husband certainly wouldn't mind. But the counter thoughts were strong: What if this were his last birthday? Don't you want to model confidence to your daughters? What if this is God telling you to do it and you don't obey? You know everyone will most likely share in your enthusiasm. You write about things you are not willing to do. Ouch. With that final thought, I took a long gulp of my beer, looked at my daughter to punctuate this moment of confidence in her brain, and said, "You asked for it." I walked half the length of the restaurant so that people on both sides of the room and on the patio could hear my request. I shouted, "Excuse me. Can I get everyone to help me sing 'happy birthday' to my husband Barrett?" And all at once, the entire room cheered, sang, and clapped. My husband looked appreciative, but my daughters' faces were awestruck. Mission accomplished.

Sometimes the best you can do is *behave as though.* I behaved as though I were the confident, radically-loving, enthusiastic woman I would naturally love to be. But not naturally being her is no excuse. There were too many possible benefits to doing the right thing, whether I felt like it or not, like honoring my husband, and maybe even God. And too much to lose in my mind: My daughters would see the coward I am. Would they be scarred for life? Probably not. They'd never even remember this day. I really wanted them to remember this day.

If you don't feel confident, act as though you are. Not all great leaders know everything, but they know who they are—growing, worthy, and capable. If the situation requires maturity, act as though you are mature while God is still growing you. Act as though you are kind until your heart has been softened. Behave as though you care as much as God would want you to. Whatever the situation calls for, if it doesn't come naturally, you can always think of what it would be like to have that trait and just do it.

SUMMARY

Twice I cried out to God to make me a better person. Twice God answered, "My grace is sufficient for thee." Not "okay." Not "I will." Not "Try harder." It was an "I gotcha." God knows what we are. Max Lucado compares us to the moon. We generate no light of our own, but how magnificent and glowing we appear at times, often receiving praise and adoration. Up close, the moon is a dusty, dark, pock-marked rock. When we reflect the light of the Son, we are magnificent and powerful, lighting the way for others through the darkness. The best version of us is the one we were created to be. When my husband knows something I don't, he remarks, "Stick with me; you'll live longer." I imagine God saying, "Stick by me; you'll shine brighter."

EXERCISE

1. List five unshakeable attributes about you.

    _____

    _____

    _____

    _____

    _____

2. List one trait you've always wished you had and practice that

trait by doing one specific behavior to that trait this month. (Maybe you've always wished you were more outgoing. Practice smiling at strangers or striking up a conversation with the checkout clerk.)

_____

_____

_____

_____

_____

A Final Note

Now That You Know

"For I am the LORD your God who takes hold of your right
hand and says to you, do not fear, I will help you."

— Isaiah 41:13

What's your next move? Maybe you've embraced acceptance for
yourself, identified your triggers, learned to speak up, felt compelled to participate more. What will you do with this internal
change? Your response is what will begin to alter your success,
confidence, and peace of mind. How will you respond? Will you
call a therapist? Apologize to someone you hurt? Sing a song of
praise? Join a team? Improve your sleep hygiene? Eat better? Quit
a bad habit? Ask for what you need? Or something else?

When my daughter completed art projects in first and second grades,
each time they looked like shit compared to those of all the other kids.
I provided all the supplies, but the work was up to her. I'm proud of
what she creates, particularly when she puts a lot of thought and time
into it. I know every time her art won't be able to compete with the
other projects that are clearly put together by a parent. It breaks my
heart to see her feel ashamed of her efforts because they don't measure
up. Sometimes I feel like a brown paper bag puppet in a world full of

papier-mâché marionettes. When we feel that way, instead of trying to compete, we can be tempted to check out. This may mean isolating, getting lost in technology, holing up, cutting off, or ending life altogether. Exposure to others can be life-threatening!

Fortunately, we also have a Father who takes pride in us how and where we are. Every day is an opportunity to sink deeper into a hole of safety from the world's promptings that we are not good enough. I do believe God's heart breaks the same way mine does as a parent. This isn't the way our existence was supposed to be. We were never meant to *think* we know bad from good. It made us judgmental, competitive, shameful, and proud. This is the fallen world we face, and we are all trying to cope with it as best we can. I truly hope that at the very least, you've taken from this book that I *get* you. I *am* you. Can I encourage you today to start healing and soothing your old wounds? Can I count on you to take a risk, and put yourself out there, even if it means getting messy?

I challenge you to write ten things here you will do over the next ninety days to claim the gift of health, peace, and growth for yourself:

1.

2.

3.

4.

5.

6.

7.

8.

9.

10.

I also want you to engage in a conversation with one person each day, whether it be a stranger, your server, your child, your boss, a coworker, or God, for one minute, where you would normally avoid engagement. Journal how it felt. Then answer the following: Was the connection deepened or loosened? Did you say something positive or encouraging? Did you receive something positive or encouraging? Did you learn something? Complete this assignment on another piece of paper or device.

You were made for more. It's time to claim that promise for yourself. I want you to be brave enough to put yourself out there. I've had the privilege of knowing God from a young age and also having therapists for best friends and coworkers most of my adult life. So, in a sense, I've always had encouragement to be my best self and the skills to make it happen at my fingertips. Above all, I have a Creator who cleans up my messes along the way and is constantly working on my behalf. I want the same for you. I'd love to hear your story and how this book applied to you, or even what felt shitty in these pages so I can improve it for the next printing. Are there any concepts I shared that you struggle to apply to your life? I'd love to offer you a complimentary, no obligation, thirty-minute phone or in-person consultation (if geography allows).

My email address is karen@karenemenheiser.com. Email me your name and time zone, and we will set up your complimentary consultation.

I wish you a life you feel good about. A life in which you feel competent and fulfilled. Be encouraged as you unbecome. You can and will come back stronger and better. I believe in you. I believe in your God.

Your friend,

Karen Emenheiser

About the Author

Karen Emenheiser grew up in the small town of Mount Joy, Pennsylvania, in a house her parents still reside in forty-seven years later. While living on the move as a Military Spouse, Karen makes yearly returns to her beloved childhood home. As a wife of sixteen years and a mother of two little girls, home is now where the Army sends her and has included Georgia, Missouri, Rhode Island, England, and currently, Hawaii.

Karen became a licensed Master's level Social Worker at the age of twenty-four, beginning her career as an in-home family therapist for families with at least one severely emotionally-disturbed child. She left this line of work after four years upon meeting her husband to commence her Military lifestyle at Fort Leonard Wood, Missouri. She switched her focus to treating the Military population and their families, namely folks returning from combat deployments during Operations Iraqi Freedom and Enduring Freedom. After six years treating trauma and helping couples through long separations and reintegrating back into their family life, Karen took a seven-year break to face a very different life challenge: stay-at-home parenting, typically managing on her own while her husband served his country in Iraq and Afghanistan. During this time, she satisfied her passion for coaching by becoming a part-time Certified Personal Trainer and Group Fitness Instructor.

When Karen's youngest child entered kindergarten, Karen immediately resumed work serving the population she is most passionate about: Service Members and their Families. Karen has been serving an Infantry Marine Corps Regiment in Hawaii, for the past three years, as their Battalions rotate in and out of six-month long deployments every eighteen months, while also serving as a senior Spouse for the United States Army. Karen is dedicated to making marriages work, helping folks find grace and inner courage, and helping them become the best versions of themselves.

Unbecoming with Karen
Heal, Move, Grow

As a gifted and educated therapist and coach, Karen draws on her years of studies, personal growth, and faith to craft an individualized plan of action with her clients to achieve a fulfilling life.

As a counselor, she has instructed and trained Military Members on resiliency, managing stress, dealing with trauma, and communicating effectively. She has worked closely with couples to help them connect on a deeper level and with individuals to tackle the beliefs that hold them back from achieving peace, joy, and harmony in their lives and relationships.

Karen speaks on various topics with a passion for moving her audience to claim their power to have a good life—now. She is eager to educate large groups and work one-on-one with folks so they can live lives of confidence.

You can hire Karen for any speaking events meant to inspire leadership and hope. Or hire her as a personal life coach and she will personally guide you on your own unique path to a more fulfilling and meaningful life, filled with taking risks and reaching goals.

To contact Karen directly, visit her website or email her:

www.KarenEmenheiser.com
karen@karenemenheiser.com